To: Chau

Enjoy!

Dorothy Brown

First Congregational Church
Eighth and D Sts. P.O. Box 248
Ramona, CA 92065-0248

THE DEAR FRANCES LETTER

by

Dorothy Brosch

authorHOUSE™

1663 LIBERTY DRIVE, SUITE 200
BLOOMINGTON, INDIANA 47403
(800) 839-8640
WWW.AUTHORHOUSE.COM

© 2005 Dorothy Brosch. All Rights Reserved.

No part of this book may be reproduced, stored in a retrieval system, or transmitted by any means without the written permission of the author.

First published by AuthorHouse 03/18/05

ISBN: 1-4208-3719-2 (e)
ISBN: 1-4208-3617-X (sc)

Printed in the United States of America
Bloomington, Indiana

This book is printed on acid-free paper.

I can tell you with my whole heart, this book would never have been written without the love, compassion, and assistance of many people. Among those whom I would like to thank, and not necessarily in this order, are the following:

> Glenn Brosch
> Gary Brosch
> Sherrie Dulworth
> Jo Anne Harvey
> Claudia Dold (editing)
> Miss Lillian
> Glen Davis
> Barbara Costella
> Martha Sparks

> My sisters:
> Alice Bryan, Sarah Schwencke, Marie Meeks

Many other friends have given me encouragement throughout the writing, editing and publishing process.

I extend my special thanks to Carolyn McKeon – www.flpw.org
of the National League of American Pen Women for her invaluable assistance.

The Dear Frances Letter is dedicated to...

...Bob's dear friend and faithful nurse who may find this book her first or last opportunity to read her letter from her patient. Bob clutched her memory deep in his heart and mind for many, many years after his chance meeting and experience with her in the St. Petersburg All Children's Hospital following his near fatal diving accident in 1949.

...To all the other "Dear Frances" caregivers, who are vital and irreplaceable. The memory of your warm hands that hold the lifeline of a patient whose world has suddenly been torn asunder and whose life has forever changed, the ray of sunshine and encouragement you offer in the darkest hour is often stored away like a warm blanket to be retrieved through the remaining days or years, as circumstances present a need for it.

...And to the powerful memory of my dear, dear friend Bob Baker.

PROLOGUE

In 1949 Bob Baker of Tampa, Florida, at the age of 15, dove into a shallow lake at a church picnic and broke his neck. He suffered a severe cervical spinal cord injury affecting all four limbs, leaving him a quadriplegic.

Bob suffered terrible (yet understandable) mood swings, going from feeling "…as low as a snake's belly" to bubbling along with a joke and a smile. However, Bob was special not **because** of his physical limitations; he was special **in spite of them**.

Bob lived through his mind, his dear friends and even brief acquaintances whose paths he graced. One of those friends was Frances, his favorite nurse in those early, dark years. In 1996 Bob wrote a letter to Frances. He had composed this in his mind, off and on for decades and he wanted to share things that he could never tell her at the time. He wanted her to know that her time with him was not wasted, and he wanted to share with her his successes. Years later, Bob shared a copy of that letter with me. After reading it, I tucked it away in a box on the top shelf of my closet. And that's where it stayed, until now.

Recently, a desire arose in me to share the story of Bob's inspiring life with others. I remembered the "Dear Frances" letter and retrieved it from its safe haven, its time-worn box tied with blue ribbon and now covered with dust. Inside the box was a brief note to me and included with it (for my pleasure) was a copy of the gardening section of a local newspaper.

The contents of the letter were originally meant for Frances, of course. The letter either never made its way into her hands, or she chose to not reply.

Using the "Dear Frances" letter as my guide and eventually my outline for this book, I gathered details from my own memories as well as those of his close friends, resulting in what I believe to be an accurate account of Bob's remarkable life.

It is my heart's desire that you will come to know through the pages of this book, the indomitable spirit of Bob Baker and his personal triumph of will over extreme physical limitations, and that in some small way, it will touch your life and maybe help others who have the misfortune of becoming a victim of life-changing accidents.

August 6*th*, 1996

My Dear Frances,

It has been my intention to bring you up to date on these many years in the form of a brief Autobiography. But the time has passed and a few infections have come and gone and my words are still running around in my head...Anyway, here goes my best (if brief) efforts using a voice activated word processor called DRAGON DICTATE!

We first met in APRIL.1949, when I was 15 plus a few months. (See photo No. 1) I stayed at Ol' Tampa Municipal Hospital for seven months, most of it on your floor. Then, came time to leave and you see the Newspaper clippings showing that sad event. Sad because I did not know what was in store for me. (See photo 2) I should have been prepared to get the "reality check" of my life!

There were many things that happened at the hospital in St. Petersburg that have had a profound and continuing effect on my life, but I won't bore you with all the details in this letter. The most important one however, was the removal of my right kidney in 1951. By the time it was diagnosed, stones had destroyed the function and it could not be saved. The very good part was that Dr. Hewit (he was with Dr. Gilmer) performed the operation and I never had a moment's problem with it again! I don't even know it's not there.

After 13 months in St. Petersburg, I was discharged into the real unknown! Coming home was very scary! Mom did not know much about taking care of me, but she gave it her very best.... And continued doing so for the next thirty-five years.... (There is a whole book to be written about this dedicated lady, but that will come later.)

At this point, I must pause and give you a tiny glimpse of my "state of mind." At that time it was Christmas Eve 1950 when I was discharged from the hospital in St. Petersburg (dumped out, would be a more accurate description"

The remainder of this letter will be interspersed in the pages of this book. The original document may be seen in its entirety in the appendix. The pictures that follow are one of Bob prior to the accident, and the other is the only picture I have of Frances.

~Bob Baker at 15 – a few months before the accident~

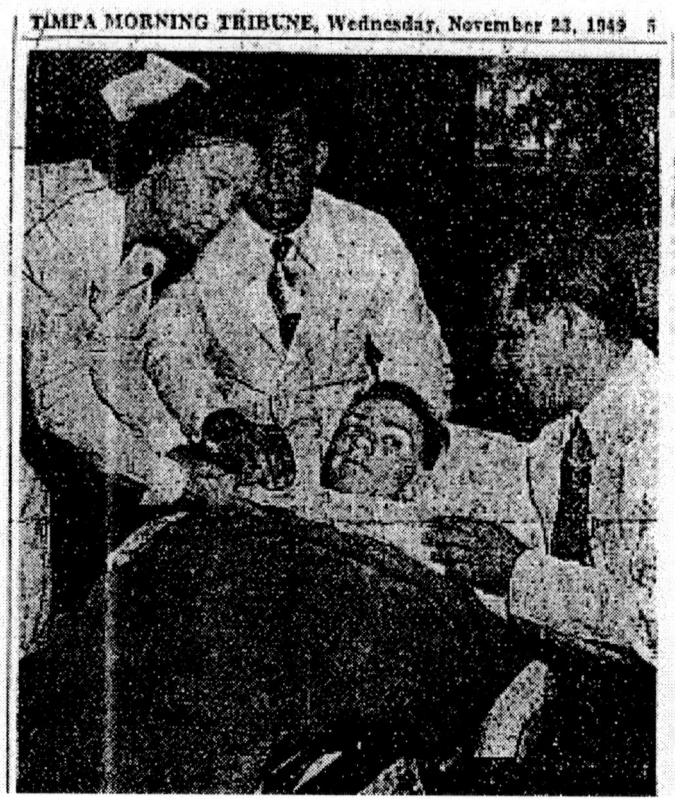

~Bob on the stretcher – on the left is his nurse Frances~

1

He lay prone on the stretcher, face down. The white sheet that covered him from the waist made his bare shoulders look big and strong. Soft blond hair framed a pair of sea-blue eyes. He was 21 or 22 years old, I guessed, and about six feet tall.

The stretcher was raised to a level for him to make eye contact with visitors when they entered the door. A pillow was placed under his chest, extending out to allow a soft surface for his elbows when he was propped up. I noticed both were bandaged tightly with what appeared to be thick layers of gauze with an ace bandage wrapped around them. I would learn later that this was to prevent pressure sores.

"So what do you want?" he asked.

"A friend told me about you and I just dropped by to get acquainted," I explained, taken aback by his abruptness. "I'm Dottie Brosch, the Director of a Recreation Program for the physically challenged here in Tampa, and I wanted to give you a personal invitation to join with us every Monday night from seven to nine. We're going to have a varied program to meet the interest and abilities of all types of people. I thought you might enjoy it."

"Humph," he snarled, as he looked at me with disgust. "And just how do you think I could join you? In case you haven't noticed, I am paralyzed. I broke my neck a few years ago in a diving accident," he explained. "It happened in 1949 when I went to a Sunday school picnic. Wish I had never gone with them to that lake."

I looked at him with compassion and dismay. Perhaps he was right, I thought, as I wondered what activity I might be able to provide for people like him who were totally paralyzed and could not even pick up something with their hands.

He seemed to be reading my mind. "But don't waste your pity on me. I can do a lot more than meets the eye."

"It must be awful to lie in bed all the time and to not be able to move. I can't begin to imagine..."

"Don't try," he interrupted, "'cause I do move."

"I don't understand."

"See that tree out there? When the wind blows the limbs and leaves, I move with them."

I looked across the room, through the door of the next room and in the distance I saw the limbs of the tree to which he had referred.

His eyes took on a dreamy look as he continued. "You'd be surprised at the things I can dream up when the wheels in my head start turning. Are you familiar with the big high bridge they are building across Tampa Bay? I read about it in the newspapers and watched on TV as it was being built. I became obsessed with a desire to see it in person. But I learned long ago that some things are out of reach for quads (Bob's shortened use of the word) so I developed some techniques all of my own; one of those tools is imagination. Now I just hop on the back of a bird flying by and tell it where to take me. This often works for me; I just imagine that it happens, as silly as it may sound to you."

"Silly!" I exclaimed. "What wonderful brain power you have. That is absolutely grand. Anyone who can dream up solutions to their problems like that has a leg up on many others who have two good arms and two workable legs. Given a choice, I would settle for your brain power any day of the week."

"Well, people who don't dream might just as well be dead," he went on with a big grin breaking across his face. "Sometime I will tell you of my really big dream. It concerns my ambition. I have it all figured out as to what I want to do with the little bit of time I have left on this earth. You may not know this but I have all ready outlived what the doctors had expected from me. Quads don't have a long life expectancy, you know."

"I didn't know that but I sure would be interested to hear about your plans. Feel like telling me now?" I settled into the hard, platform rocker and awaited his answer.

"For openers," he began, "I will find some way to build or buy a big brick home with plenty of windows in my room. I want to see either the sun come up in the morning or go down in the evening; I have almost forgotten what that looks like. I will hire nurses to work around the clock to cut down on my mother's workload. I am getting too big for her to handle," he boasted. "I can't do a thing for myself. She has to feed me and bathe me and turn me every two hours to keep down pressure sores. I'm really a load for her to take care of by herself."

While he was talking I surveyed the immaculately clean room. There were only two small windows, one of which was blocked with the small air conditioner that was whirring away as if struggling to get air. A slatted blind hung from the other window. His stretcher and a stainless steel table seemed to consume most of the room. A small army cot lined one wall, neatly made up with sheets and a pillow that still had the imprint of his mother's head where she had slept the night before. A single faded platform rocker and a tiny footstool with needlepoint cover was parallel to the third wall, leaving only space for a medium sized wicker basket filled with odds and ends of knitting threads. The floor was covered with worn linoleum that was clean enough to eat off of. His bed was centered, facing the door.

"Well, Bob," I said, "With wheels in the head like you say you have and with dreams like yours, there will be no stopping you. With your determination, good things are going to happen. I know your dream will come true. Just keep the faith," I told him softly.

"Faith!" he shouted at me. "What has faith got to do with it? Don't go preaching to me."

I stared at him in disbelief as he went on to tell me he did not believe there was a God. And if there was, He could not be a just and loving God. "I didn't do anything to deserve this. Why would He let this happen to me?"

I was too stunned to give him a quick reply. Finally, searching his angry eyes for understanding, I admitted that I didn't have all the answers. I too didn't know why.

"Well, thanks anyway, for not giving me a bunch of fiddle-de-dee answers," he said, calming down.

While staring hard into my eyes, he suddenly asked, "Who are you, anyhow? And what do you want with me? Are you a therapist?"

I smiled at the suggestion before answering with a firm "no."

"A nurse?" he asked.

"Wrong again."

"Bet you are from a church," he persisted.

"No, Bob. As I told you before, I am a recreation director. I work with the City of Tampa Recreation Department and I am trying to organize a recreation program for disabled people. We are meeting the recreational needs of most of our citizens, but before now, we offered nothing for people like you. And I feel that you and others with similar challenges should have some fun too."

"Well, what makes you think you can teach me how to have fun? Can you show me how to ride my bike and deliver papers again? Can you show me how to take my girl to the movies or to play soccer?"

He stared defiantly at me.

As my eyes swept over him I could not help but stare at the long, healthy-looking form lying under the tightly fitted sheet and I pondered the things he had told me. They seemed to have come from the depth of his soul. I thought about his big dreams and plans for his future.

"Don't you think you would enjoy being around more people instead of being shut in all the time?"

"Look, Lady," he snorted. "Let's get this over with. For your information, I have not been out of this house for five years except when I went to see the doctors and besides, I wouldn't be able to do anything if I did go. Obviously you don't know much about quadriplegia."

"No, I'm afraid I don't know much about quadriplegia," I admitted.

"Well, don't feel bad about that. Very few people know how to spell it, and even fewer know what it does to the human psyche. So you're not alone in that."

"I'm not interested in what you can't do, Bob," I injected. "I'm just interested in what you CAN do."

"It would be foolish for me to go to a recreation center and frankly, I am not interested." I felt like a pendulum on a grandfather clock as I tried to keep up with his mood swings. While searching for the right thing to say, I blurted out: "How long are you, anyway?" (I had meant to ask how long he had been in this condition.)

"What a stupid question" he exclaimed. "I WAS six feet TALL before my accident and I guess I still am. That is tall, mind you, and don't say I'm long. I can tell already that you are looking at my condition and not seeing the real me."

I saw my mistake and my words hung in the air between us.

"I'm sorry, Bob", I quickly replied. I rose to my feet and prepared to leave. "I'd better be going now, but I really am glad to have met you."

"Yea, I'll bet."

"Hope to see you again soon." I could see he was still angry.

"Mom and I never did like do-gooders anyway," I heard him say into his pillow as I turned to leave.

"Do-gooder!" I exclaimed. "What do you mean?"

"Aw, you know. We get do-gooders coming by all the time. Gives them something to talk about when they go out with friends. They always ask what they can do for me, yet it would never cross their minds to offer to sit with me.and give Mom some time away from chores or to do the shopping for her. She has too much to do, but little do they know what it means to be shut in with no one to help out."

"Do-gooder!" I exclaimed, turning to face him again. "Is that what you think I am?" He grinned at me, knowing he had bested me.

I had gone but a few steps when I heard him say in a gentle voice, "Call before you come the next time."

I walked to my car with tears flowing freely from my eyes. How sad that such a handsome, smart fellow was so helpless. Over and over again I heard those awful words, "do-gooder", and I did a quick personal analysis. *Was he right? Why did I think I could teach people like him to have fun?*

But after all, fun was my business. Maybe I should just be satisfied to help able-bodied people. I was good at that; I should let well enough alone and forget this idea of a truly recreational program for the physically challenged.

2

I went to the recreation center on Monday evening several weeks later to start our first program. I wondered if anybody would show up, or if I had wasted all my spare time for the past weeks following up on referrals. And if they did come, as many whom I had contacted had promised, would I be able to provide a program that would hold their interest?

Basketball courts surrounded the huge, unpainted concrete block building, known as *The Rec*. A six-foot chain link fence separated the play area from the parking lot. I had admired the ugly old building the first time I had seen it for I knew the labor of love and hope that had been poured into it. The families in the community had gone from door to door seeking donations from local merchants in order to finance its construction. In sharing the cost of the big project, the ladies cooked and sold spaghetti dinners, held fish fries, conducted bake sales and auctioned concrete blocks. The men donated their labor and supported the efforts of their wives by selling tickets to the dinners and buying blocks at one dollar apiece. The front end of the building was reserved for a community health clinic. The remainder of the building was used for nightly recreation programs for all age groups, from preteens to senior citizens.

I was encouraged to see the lady from the ceramic shop that I had phoned earlier in the week. She was waiting patiently at the door wearing a big smile. A bibbed apron, smudged with dried clay and dabs of paint, covered most of her wheelchair. She had come straight from her ceramic shop to help us out.

"I have all of the supplies in my van to do ceramics tonight," she said happily." I thought it would be fun starting with raw clay instead of green ware. Almost everybody likes to play with clay and get their hands dirty."

"Wonderful!" I exclaimed. "Come on in!"

I watched with pride as Gladys, our volunteer ceramic teacher, rolled her chair up the newly-built ramp. We entered the big auditorium together and my eyes swept down the long, blank wall lined with tables for four. The chairs had been placed neatly nearby but away from the tables to allow convenient access for the wheel chairs. Across the back of the long room was a fifty-foot stage camouflaged by a huge, beige draw drape that flowed gracefully from ceiling to floor hiding the single pieces of furniture, a piano and stool.

My eyes continued across the opposite wall and I noted, as if for the first time, the four small windows above eye level, under which was a large, red soda machine standing beside the long, curved refreshment bar. This served the duel purpose of being a storage place for records and the portable player. I walked beside her wheelchair to the record counter. On hearing that the music had stopped, I started looking for a different record. I was taken aback by a man's voice directly behind me.

"Hey lady!" his big voice boomed. "Hand me that record!"

I automatically reached behind the music counter and picked up the record, Elvis' *Blue Suede Shoes*, which had just finished playing. I turned to give it to the owner of the big voice, and was so startled I began to shake.

The "voice" came from a young man, in his late teens, who had no hands and no arms, just a torso. I stood there in shock, holding the record out to the young man with no arms.

"Gotcha, didn't I?" Doug said, enjoying the joke he had pulled on me. He maneuvered his shoulders to spin himself around like a top in his chair. I felt faint when I saw he had no legs, either. He was enjoying the prank that he obviously had used many times before to break the shock when people first saw him. In spite of being very nervous and upset, I noticed that people all around me were laughing. And quite a few people had arrived by this time. It seemed each one had brought a friend, family member, or an attendant with them. The place was becoming crowded.

"I'm not a do-gooder after all," I thought proudly, as I struggled to regain my composure. These people are thrilled to be out of their home and around others with similar circumstances and conditions.

The recorded music stopped later, and someone opened the drapes. All eyes turned to face the lady playing the piano on the stage. They stared with delight at the beautiful middle-aged lady playing the old time favorites. When I introduced her, there was a big round of applause.

Then, while introducing Sandy, her Seeing Eye dog lying quietly at her feet, the crowd went wild with appreciation. It was only at that moment they realized she was blind. Music soon filled the room and I watched and listened as different voices began to emerge.

"Aha!" I thought, "We have the makings of a choral group already!"

I noted my new friend, Doug, was singing his heart out to everyone's delight. His booming voice almost drowned out those nearest him. Another activity was born, I thought, watching while almost everybody began to sing.

On the other side of the room, lying flat on his back on a wheelchair that looked like a stretcher with oversized wheels, was a man named Lamont Spriggs, of rather large build, singing along with the tune *My Wild Irish Rose*. I learned later that this was the only position in which he could be. His attendant, dressed in white, had brought him from the county home and hospital.

By his side was a hand-crafted wooden crate on wheels containing a little man whose body was no more than two feet long and which lay frozen in a permanent "S" position. Even though he had recently been shaved, black stubble spread over his tiny face like rye grass just beginning to sprout. He wasn't singing, but he wore a giant smile, and his jet-black eyes were shining like diamonds. He was enjoying every minute.

His name was Tony Gonzalez, but he was called "Little Tony. " When we first met at the hospital, I had asked him where he lived. He said he lived right there… at the county home and hospital. When he saw my quizzical look, he went on to explain that when he was just a little fellow his parents had grown tired of people asking, "What is it?" as they pushed him down the street in his crate on wheels. When his parents could no longer endure such cruel remarks, they had left him there, crate and all, outside the front door of the hospital.

He didn't get out much, he had told me, but he sure had a lot of friends who had visited him over the past 34 years since he had been in the County Home. "They are real good to me," he said, smiling at his attendant who returned the smile with much fondness.

Across the room, I met the friendly gray eyes of very tall man sitting in a wheel chair. He was breathing with the help of a portable respirator. I inched my way through the crowd to his side and introduced myself and welcomed him warmly. He told me his name was Lester Rosenblatt, but his friends called him Les and that he couldn't stay long as he could only be out of his iron lung for two hours at a time. He had heard about this program and wanted to come out and see what it was all about.

> *I was 16 with very little past, almost no present and (from my point of view) absolutely no future. No real education! No money! No goals! And, no way visible to attain any of these things.*
>
> *In the next five years or so, I tried to finish high school by correspondence study, but without a goal that resulted only in a GED diploma. (See photo #3) I tried a number of other things without much success – and in the spring of 1956, a very fortuitous and wonderful thing happened!*
>
> *I was invited to join a recreation group for handicapped people and there I met a wonderful and enthusiastic woman whose name is Dorothy Brosch. (There will be a lot more about this amazing lady in future letters, but that part of*

my story will fill another book by itself.) Just by chance, she introduced me to Les Rosenblatt who was to become my first business associate – and over the next twenty years went on {to} become a strong friend, a wise mentor and would help me form most of my basic business philosophies.

Lester explained briefly that he had had polio. It was interesting to hear that he was in the insurance business and able to support himself. I congratulated him and told him about the young fellow, Bob, whom I had just recently met. I explained that they seemed to have similar problems, even though Bob's paralysis had been caused by a diving accident. He invited me to drop by his office to visit, as he would like to hear more about the young man. I happily agreed, as I wanted to know more about how he managed a business with his disability.

3

I called his office the next day and was greeted with a friendly voice that told me to "Hold, please while I connect you with my boss."

"Hi, Les," I began, "I'm Dottie Brosch, the director of the program you attended last night and I was wondering when it would be convenient for me to drop by for a short visit?"

"Well," he hesitated, "Everything I do is on a tight time schedule but right now would be just perfect. Can you make it?"

"Give me 30 minutes," I answered happily.

"I'll be waiting to see you," he said, leaving no mistake in my mind that he was as happy as I was about us meeting again.

I drove as fast as I dared for I knew every thing he did was timed and I was eager to talk with him. His office was inside a neat little bungalow on a main street. When I entered the door with the "Welcome" sign, an attractive lady sitting at a desk in a glassed in area greeted me. She spoke through a small opening in the glass and told me to go on back through the door to my right. I could see through the half opened door, to the big iron lung and Les sitting very erect in a wheel chair beside it. He was expecting me, and was smiling broadly as he welcomed me into his office. Then, into the intercom resting on his shoulder he drawled, "Hold all my calls, Mary."

I noted that none of this had required the use of his hands, both of which lay still in front of him.

It didn't take long for Les to explain that he had contracted polio a few years back and had been forced to close his insurance business until he could make the necessary adaptations that would allow him to conduct his business. I was awed with the creative manner in which he had worked out his challenges.

There was a phone resting on his right shoulder, fastened with a unique clip that kept it secure while he answered or made his business contacts. "Mary, my secretary, supplies the arms and legs needed," he told me with a boyish grin.

I made a mental note of the writing pen strapped on his hand with tape. He followed my eyes and explained "This enables me put my *X* on the dotted lines."

Time passed all too quickly and I left with a promise to return for another visit soon. I was grinning when I turned my car toward the home of my new challenge, Bob. I could hardly wait to tell him about Les and to show him how he might be able to work out some similar methods to meet his own needs. Les had offered to assist Bob in any way possible, as he could well recall how tough it had been for him when he started adjusting to his own paralysis.

4

Bob's mother met me at the door with a warm smile. "Bob told me he called you a" Do-Gooder" when you were here before." She offered an apology for his behavior. "We have to accept whatever he dishes out though, for he has been through so much." She invited me to join her in the kitchen where she was making Bob's lunch.

"I'm sure he has been through a lot," I told her, "And you too," I added while looking at her thin little body and face which was marked deeply with stress lines and fatigue.

"Nobody will ever know just how hard it is to have a big, healthy son one day and then to be left with THAT," she sighed, looking through the door toward Bob's room. I felt myself cringe and hoped that Bob lying in the next room had not heard the remark. I followed her to the little kitchen, noting that this part of the house had no air-conditioning.

She started telling about his diving accident that happened when he was only 15 years of age. He had played soccer on the Church's team the morning on that fateful day and later in the afternoon, had joined the group for a picnic and swim.

She had been working in her garden all morning before the awful phone call came telling her of Bob's accident at the lake. She remembers grabbing her purse and racing wildly in her car to go to his side.

"The rest," she said, "was like a bad dream."

She told me about how she had stared at her soiled hands while riding with Bob in the ambulance to the hospital and wishing that she could at least have had time to wash them. She would never forget the look of pain on her son's pale face, which was as white as the sheet that covered him on the stretcher.

She pulled out the little straight chair from the table in the kitchen and invited me to sit down and have coffee with her. She filled our cups almost to overflowing while her mind seemed to go elsewhere.

Finally, she continued with the story of Bob's accident, giving many details of the horrors she had experienced throughout the next few days and nights as they operated on him and did a multitude of procedures, trying to save his life and maintain as much mobility as possible.

But the reports grew worse as the days passed. She could only visit him for short intervals in the Critical Care Unit. She wiped a tear with the back of her hand, remembering, and finally went on.

August, 1953. It has been four years since my accident and the kid is still looking and feeling apprehensive! And the next great adventure is about to begin. I was being sent by the Baptist organization for an {sic} physical evaluation that was only four years late. The destination was the hallowed halls of medicine at New York University Medical Center in New York City, New York, U.S.A. Now, with a name like that you might assume they would know everything about rehabilitation. The only problem was that in those days nobody knew much about putting a broken body back together. They knew how to spell rehabilitation and that was about it! Heck, I had delusions of walking out of that place in a couple of weeks. Needless to say, I was crushed to learn they had nothing to offer.

AUGUST, 1953. IT HAS BEEN FOUR YEARS SINCE MY ACCIDENT AND THE KID IS STILL LOOKING AND FEELING APPREHENSIVE! AND THE NEXT GREAT ADVENTURE IS ABOUT TO BEGIN. I WAS BEING SENT BY THE BAPTIST ORGANIZATION FOR AN PHYSICAL EVALUATION THAT WAS ONLY FOUR YEARS LATE. THE DESTINATION WAS THE HALLOWED HALLS OF MEDICINE AT NEW YORK UNIVERSITY MEDICAL CENTER IN NEW YORK CITY, NEW YORK, U. S. A.. NOW, WITH A NAME LIKE THAT YOU MIGHT ASSUME THEY WOULD KNOW EVERYTHING ABOUT REHABILITATION. THE ONLY PROBLEM WAS THAT IN THOSE DAYS NOBODY KNEW MUCH ABOUT PUTTING A BROKEN BODY BACK TOGETHER. THEY KNEW HOW TO SPELL REHABILITATION AND THAT WAS ABOUT IT! HECK, I HAD DELUSIONS OF WALKING OUT OF THAT PLACE IN A COUPLE OF WEEKS. NEEDLESS TO SAY, I WAS CRUSHED TO LEARN THEY HAD NOTHING TO OFFER!

IN THIS PICTURE, THE LADY IN THE BLACK DRESS IS MOM, WITH A FRIEND OF THE FAMILY ON EACH SIDE. JUST MOM AND I WENT ON THIS ADVENTURE, AS WE DID ON MOST ADVENTURES IN THE YEARS TO COME.

Seven months after his accident, the attending physicians in Tampa decided to send him to a hospital in New York, for they had determined that all four limbs were paralyzed and that he needed more specialized care and therapy than they were able to give him.

His mother had lived those months in a little rented room nearby the hospital so she could visit him as often as possible. She smiled when she spoke of having to walk a few blocks to the nearest store to buy some clothes until her husband could mail a package to her from home.

"Excuse me," she said, as she angrily attacked a small carrot on the cutting board. She was making chicken soup for their lunch.

"I have to cut every thing so small" she said, apologizing for the noise. "It's easier for him to drink through a straw than for me to feed him with a spoon. Soup is nourishing, you know, and also cheap because I can boil the bones twice. We have had a time making ends meet", she explained. "The bill collectors have just about driven me crazy." I wiped a few tears from my eyes, hoping all the while that she wouldn't notice.

She turned the burner on low and we sipped our coffee as she continued her sad story. As it unraveled, I found myself feeling her pain since I had two sons of my own. One was about the same age as Bob. She squared her shoulders and rose to her feet when she noticed I had finished my coffee.

"We'd better go see Bob before he gets mad at us. He says I always hog up his company," she finished with a gentle smile.

He was propped up on his elbows smiling broadly when we entered the room. At first glance one would not think anything was wrong with him.

"I had hoped you would come back", he said softly, "And I'm sorry I called you a do-gooder."

He told me of the many well wishers who were forever coming to see him saying how sorry they were about his accident. But they, in spite of offering to assist any way possible, couldn't see that a simple offer to sit with him while his mother. went to the store, or to help her do the dishes, would have meant so much to her. Now that is what I call a Do-gooder," He went on." And, you know something? You did me a favor. You stared at my legs under the cover and it reminded me that I still had legs. I sometimes forget, you know."

I assured him that I had already forgotten about his calling me a do-gooder. He rewarded me with one of the warmest smiles I had ever seen. His teeth were shiny white and beautifully even.

"Besides, I have lots to tell you about our first program last night" I said hurriedly, trying to make my point before his mood changed.

His eyes looked at me, pleadingly, "Please understand that I would love to take part in your program, but I simply can't. There are too many problems and Mother has more than she can handle without me adding to her load. There is no way we could afford an ambulance to provide my transportation, and we don't even have a ramp. There's just no way I could go out just for my own pleasure."

"I have a friend who owns a funeral home," I quickly told him, "and he has said he would send one of his ambulances to pick you up and then return you to your home afterwards."

"My goodness," he exclaimed. "For a few minutes, I wondered what a funeral had to do with me. I have been close enough to needing one, but I am doing quite well right now thank you Ma'am." he said with a chuckle.

"And as for a ramp, that is the least of our worries." I told him about the group of volunteers who had been helping us. They had already built the ramp at the center and I felt certain they would help us again.

I detected a sign of interest. Words tumbled from my mouth so fast I hardly knew what I was saying. I went on to tell him about the conditions of some of the participants who had come out for the first program. I assured him that some seemed to be in more dire conditions than he.

"Huh!" he snorted doubtfully.

"Some were able to walk and some required ambulances," I told him, "but the majority used wheel chairs." He stared at me in disbelief.

I told him about Lester Rosenblatt, who was not only a quadriplegic but used an iron lung at home and a portable respirator when he went out. I told Bob about the intercom being on one shoulder and the phone on the other, and how he had his secretary do the legwork while he sold insurance via telephone. He wanted to hear more. I tried to explain how he used a pencil taped to his hand to dial the phone. Apparently, he had the same limited movement of the lower arms, but, like Bob, he could not use his hands.

When I told him I had to go, he begged me to stay. He wanted to hear more about Les.

"Bob, you simply must come to the Center and meet him," I implored. "Say you will, and just leave the rest of the arrangements to me."

"We'll see," he agreed, doubtfully.

The volunteers showed up at Bob's home the next day and the ramp was built in short order. They even wheeled him outside on his stretcher so he could supervise the job.

I was getting ready to go to work when my phone rang. It was Bob. He couldn't wait to call and tell me about his ramp and to thank me for helping to make it possible. I felt good, oh, how very good! Thank the Lord for volunteers!

"The ambulance will pick you up at 6:30 next Monday evening, okay?"

"You bet," he exclaimed. "Mother will have me ready for them. And, by the way, thanks a lot". I could all but see his smile through the phone and I could certainly hear it in his voice.

The next call was to Les. I explained what had happened with Bob and asked if he would please make an effort to come to the center on Monday night. It would help Bob so much for them to get acquainted since their conditions were so similar.

"Well," he hesitated. "I can't promise, as you know my condition. But, the Good Lord willing, I will give it my best shot."

The rest of the week flew by as I made more contacts and planned activities for the second program.

5

The parking spaces at the Center filled up fast, as many volunteers, Red Cross vehicles, commercial ambulances, county hospital personnel and families delivered the people. Bob wore a grin that covered his face from ear to ear when he arrived in a commercial ambulance. But I could see at first glance that he was a bit nervous and somewhat skeptical.

"Place him beside the man on the respirator," I told the attendant, making certain that Bob could talk to Lester without wasting any time.

After introducing them, I left them alone, for I knew they would have a lot to talk about. I became absorbed in directing the activities and didn't notice that Les had left the room until a short while later.

"Where's Les?" I asked Bob, after going quickly to his side.

"He said he had to go. But he invited me to go visit him sometime at his office. I doubt that would ever be possible, but I really enjoyed talking with him" Bob explained happily.

"Who knows?" I answered. "We'll have to work on that."

It wasn't long before a lovely, blond lady named Jan wheeled herself over to sit by Bob and I noted how quickly they became engaged in conversation. Soon they were both laughing.

Bob was one happy camper when he was telling us goodbye. "I'll be back next Monday" he grinned meeting my eye. "I had a wonderful time. Thanks for everything, and call me when you have time."

I called Bob the next day to get his reaction to the program. He was ecstatic and asked if I would be able to come by that same afternoon. I asked if the next day would be all right as I had so much to do.

"I have a girl friend," he boasted. "I met her at the Center. Her name is Jan. We made a date to sit together next Monday night. I can't wait to tell you about her. She called me up this morning."

It was raining when I arrived at Bob's home the next day. His mother met me at the car with an umbrella.

"Bob told me to have it ready for you so you wouldn't get wet. I don't know what happened at the Center, but Bob hasn't been the same since he came home."

"How's that?" I smiled knowingly.

"He's so happy!" she exclaimed. "Normally, I can't do anything to please him, but since he went out there, I haven't done anything wrong."

She left us alone and Bob started right in talking about Les and his newfound girlfriend. He had loved the program but most of all, everybody had been so friendly.

"And not one person tried to shake my hand when we met," he exclaimed. "That is what I had feared the most. You see," he said, lifting his arm to the elbow, and looking sadly at his hands, "They are just like dead fish. I used to have spasms in my hands and when my fingers rubbed over the sheets, it caused pressure sores. The doctors finally decided to cut the tendons so I would have no more problems with them. They wanted to operate on my feet too, but Mother wouldn't agree to it...they even considered amputating my feet, but that threw Mom into a purple rage."

"But please get rid of that frown on your face," he said, "That's the facts, Lady," he added with a grin, "Just the plain facts of my life."

"Well, tell me about this girl you met," I said, hoping to change the subject.

He spent the next ten minutes or so talking about how wonderful she was and that they had made a date for the next meeting. His eyes fairly danced as he related how she had asked if she could sit by him at the next meeting and that she was a beautiful blond named Jan and that he had loved talking with her because she made him feel so good. She had a spinal problem from birth and had never walked.

"Gee," he exclaimed sadly. "It must be awful to have never walked. Just think, I was walking up until my accident. At least, I know what it feels like to walk."

The next outing for Bob was even better than the last. He was a great conversationalist and a group had gathered around him to listen and participate. Jan was, as before, right at his side. Her mother and father stood nearby enjoying the sight of their only daughter's obvious happiness. Bob and Jan were oblivious to the people around them and soon were engaged in a conversation all of their own.

"I'll see you soon," he said, directing his remark at me as he was being wheeled out to the ambulance to return to his home.

I talked with his attendant earlier, and asked if there was any chance of getting them to transport Bob to pay a short visit with Les sometime soon, in the daytime. They told me they would gladly work at no charge for their time, and they thought they could make arrangements with the owner to use his ambulance.

6

And what a big day that was! Bob's mother had him ready and the attendants rolled him down his own ramp and away they went to visit Les. His mother told me later that Bob had been so excited she had trouble containing him.

When my phone rang, I just knew it was Bob calling. I had watched the clock. I knew he had had time to get back home.

"You will never guess what happened!" he all but shouted in my ear. "Les offered to help me get into the insurance business if I can get Rehab to provide the course and text books and study real hard. He said I could even do my internship in his office with him if I could figure some way to get there."

His voice lowered as he went on, "If, if, if…that seems to be what my life is made up of these days. And, some of those *ifs* are almost insurmountable."

"Like what?" I asked.

"For openers, Rehab is pretty disgusted with me. After they helped me get my GED a few years ago, they offered me other assistance that I refused. No doubt they were left with a bad taste in their mouths when they found me to be such a pain to get along with."

"But, we can work that out," I assured him. "What else?"

"Transportation is a big one. We sure don't have any money to take care of that. Les said I would have to intern with a licensed broker at least once a week for several months, to get my own license and that would be impossible."

"Let's cross that bridge when we get to it," I said matter-of-factly, as if all we had to do was wave a magic wand and all of our wishes would come true.

I promised to intervene with Rehabilitation for him, wondering how on earth these arrangements could be made.

To my relief, when I made the phone call, the man at Rehabilitation was delighted to hear that Bob had taken an interest in something after all this time and he promised to get on Bob's case right away.

Then I worried about how we could work this out for him. After all, he could not even turn the pages of the books. His mother was already burdened with having to give all the special care that he needed and doing the neighbor's laundry each week to supplement their meager income.

Bob's father had deserted them a few months after Bob had come home from the hospital. Having grown exasperated with seeing his only son and fishing companion in this condition, Bob's father had simply walked away from them. He had told them the day he left that he simply couldn't tolerate any more of the bill collectors that were constantly pestering them. He had been unable to get a job and Bob's mother was forever fussing at him to get out and find something to do.

Both Bob and his mother had cried the day he left, they had told me earlier, although they both had agreed that it was one less person for her to feed and to wait on, and there would be fewer arguments from him to put up with. Times had been real rough, back then, they both had agreed.

When I called to tell Bob that a man from the Rehabilitation Office would be out to see about signing him up for the course, he could hardly believe it. Neither he nor his mother thought they would give him another chance. They were so pleased and said they could hardly wait to get started.

Bob called later to tell me he had his insurance course and was ready to start studying. I rushed over to his house and we examined the books together. We noted that at the end of each chapter were questions and answers. The instructor had suggested he study the pages thoroughly and then work the questions and answers so he could be certain he had understood it all.

Without even the slightest movement of his head or neck, but a simple rising of his eyebrows, he raised his eyes from the book and looked at me when it was time to turn a page. We completed the first chapter and I was amazed at how thoroughly he had digested its contents. We laughed about it and I promised to come back the next day on my way to work to study the second chapter with him. This went on day after day for several months With the help of his mother in the evenings, he made rapid progress.

I discovered that I could leave my house one hour and a half early on my way to work to study with him. We had many hours of fun when we were together and ended each session by exchanging personal tidbits about our lives. It was on one of these days that I asked Bob about the old-fashioned hat rack that stood in the corner of his room, loaded with hats and caps of every description.

"All of those hat yours?"

'They sure are," he answered, proudly. "I have always liked hats and caps and I had a small collection of them before my accident."

"That's interesting, Bob."

"Yeah, some of my friends keep giving them to me as gifts now, and I love every one of them. And would you believe I still wear them?"

"You do?" I asked in surprise.

"Yeah, when I get thoroughly bored, just lying around, I often look at those hats and eventually am able to conjure up a vision of wearing one of them to a ball game or going fishing with my Dad, or just whatever strikes my fancy at that time. It also helps me to think of the friend who gave it to me and on what occasion the hat was given." He lowered his eyes shyly, looking much like a little boy caught with his hand in the cookie jar. "Gee, Dottie, I don't want to bore you with all this stuff."

"Well, it certainly isn't boring to me," I assured him. "How about telling me about some of them?" I walked across the room to the hat tree and lifted one up for him to see. "This sure is an interesting one."

"Yeah, that is one of my favorites," He was grinning broadly with happy memories. "It's a Mississippi River Gambler's hat."

"For goodness sake," I exclaimed, admiring its high dome-like crown and narrow brim and the feathered hat band tied around it.

"A friend brought that back to me after making a trip to New Orleans. That was given to me in 1953, not too long after my accident," he added.

Seeing his pleasure in his collection, I urged him to tell me more. To my surprise, he had names and approximate dates for almost each one. He pointed out the Stetson, and the English tweed hat and on down the line to his Dad's fishing hat..

When we had finished examining the hats I said to him, "You amaze me, Bob. No wonder I like to visit with you so much. There's never a dull moment when you're around."

He focused once more on the hat tree. "I even wear that fur lined job when I go on imaginary trips up north with my friends."

"That's what I call using your head to make things happen."

He laughed out loud, and then as quickly, became solemn again."I often think of myself as 'the head' as that is all I feel and have control of now." His eyes held mine as he obviously hoped for my understanding.

Dorothy Brosch

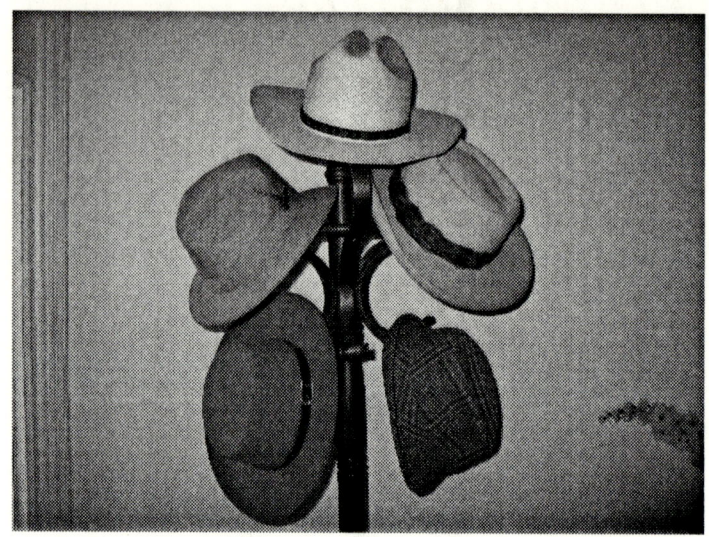

In the meantime, he appeared at the Recreation Center every Monday to meet with his friends. He was very popular from the onset. The ladies were all trying to be first in line to talk with him and to sit by him. They listened avidly when he told them of his plans to take a correspondence course in insurance and many wondered how he could manage such an undertaking in his condition.

I couldn't help but wonder what his secret charm was. Was it his big, innocent blue eyes, or was it his constant big smile? After months of close observation, I realized he focused on each person he spoke with, giving them his undivided attention. He wasn't shy about asking questions, but the biggest thing of all was that he listened and heard their replies. People always left him with an elevated feeling of self-importance.

We were all surprised, one night a few weeks later, when he appeared sitting upright in a wheelchair. When the attendants pushed his chair up the ramp, the entire crowd seemed to take one big gasp. He gave me an especially big smile as he came near. "About time I used my chair, don't you think?" he asked between chuckles. His mother had come with him and she was beaming like a new bride. She explained that he had been practicing sitting up for several weeks and she had come along just to make sure he didn't get too tired. She stood by his side while he introduced her to his new friends, then she left to visit with some of the other family members.

It was a pleasure for me to watch, as some would work ceramics and sing or hum along with the piano music in the background. At another big table in the room, a group had formed to do bead work and other crafts. The program at the center had been running for several months when an Advisory Council, comprised of participants of the group, decided they should make it a club instead of a program. They also wanted to elect a slate of officers to conduct monthly meetings. We didn't see much politicking going on, but when election night arrived they all seemed to know who they wanted to be the president of their club.

Bob was elected unanimously. He admitted later to being afraid of the task before him, but had not known how to say no.

"But," he went on, "as long as Jan is my secretary, I think I can do it." He confessed that Jan was the first girl he had been interested in since his accident. Although confined to a wheel chair, Jan was confident and satisfied with herself. She wore a perpetual smile and had a ready, hearty laugh for any occasion. She always wore bright clothes that seemed to match and enhance her bubbly personality.

"I just enjoy looking at her," Bob once confessed. "I find myself looking in her eyes that never stopped twinkling and staring at her full red smiling lips, and I wonder what would happen if one day she surprised me by planting them tight against my own lips. I wonder if she wears that smile even in her sleep," he finished with a grin.

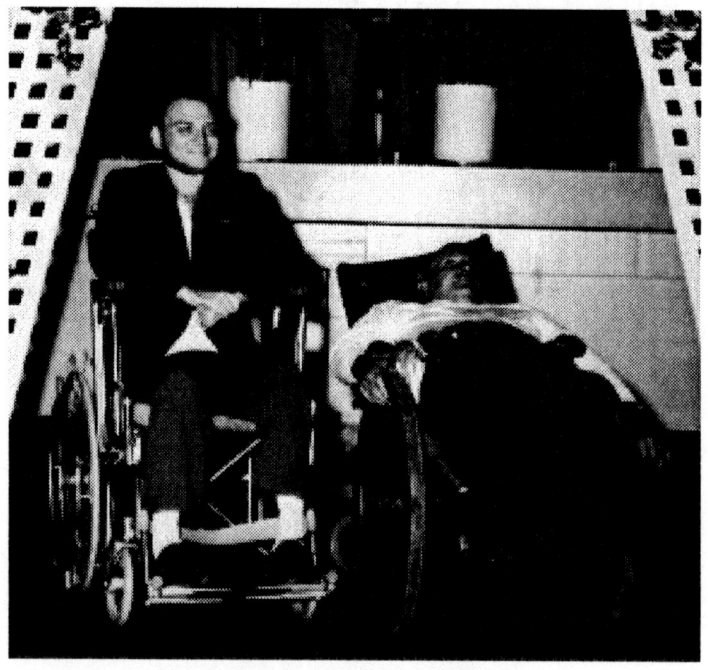

~Bob and Lamont Spriggs~

Often awed by Bob's confessions, I seldom knew how to answer them. I learned to just listen, as so many times it was as if he didn't expect an answer.

One day he explained to me in no uncertain terms that he may be totally paralyzed, but that didn't mean that his desire to be with a pretty woman was paralyzed. "I believe that 95% of physical desire and passion is in one's head anyway, and there's nothing wrong with my head," he laughed.

"Well, thank the Good Lord for that anyway, Bob." I had replied lamely.

"Yeah," he quickly agreed, "but I wish..." leaving the sentence hanging in mid-air.

"You wish what, Bob?"

"I just wish people could know and understand that all the feeling I have in my body is from my neck up." I made a mental note to always touch him on his face or head each time I was with him. But, it also left me wondering where he got his passion for Jan? I was satisfied with his explanation that it came from his mind.

When Jan entered the room each Monday night, accompanied with her Mom and Dad, people around Bob automatically made room for her by his side. The two became almost a spectator event as their brilliant minds joined, collided and at times clashed.

Their laughter echoed through the large room and served as a magnet drawing others nearer to take part in the action.

Since Jan was already acquainted with most of the people, she lost no time in making certain that Bob learned each of their names. Some kind soul wrote down the names of each of the members and listed their phone numbers for him. Maybe Jan felt that was part of her newly acquired secretarial duties.

I learned later that Bob spent many of his evenings contacting each member and learning all he could about them and their problems. He took their problems as his own and with his clear thinking mind he began having counseling sessions with them. He would make as many calls as necessary to help solve their problems according to their severity. He would often entrust me with their worries and get my opinion on what they should do or whom they could contact for help.

In no time, Bob had forgotten his own problems. His had become small in comparison to theirs, he soon decided.

Some of them were homeless and had no family. One lady had an incurable disease that she had been told would get progressively worse, leaving her only a short time to live. She and her little daughter had been living in the Projects with her aging mother. She wanted to make arrangements for her little girl's future before her time ran out.

Bob was appalled at the hopelessness they faced and was determined to do something about it if he could. People in the club knew that they could get a straight answer from Bob and could trust him with their innermost problems. He was soon endeared into the hearts of all the people in the club as more and more confided in him and sought his advice.

7

While our ceramic teacher, Gladys, was scrounging through her studio one day, she discovered a small mold for making earrings. The mold, the size of a saucer, had six little places to make different kinds of leaves. Thinking that some of the ladies in the club would be interested in doing this, she placed them in the stack of supplies to be carried to the program that night. When she showed it to me, my heart jumped for joy. I had a brainstorm. Little Tony could make these.

Tony laughed when I posed the idea to him, showing him the molds. "What on earth would I do with earrings?"

I suggested he make them for the nurses at the County Home and Hospital. He waited patiently while we folded a towel over his body to catch any dripping. Then, we took a small wad of clay and rolled it between our palms until it was the size of a marble. With his one moveable thumb, he pressed and he pressed the ball into the mold of a maple leaf. We held the mold just under his hand that always stuck up in the air. His thumb moved very slowly but finally the little ball was flat. We very carefully removed it from the mold and held the perfect maple leaf up for Tony to see.

"Hmm," he said with a smile, "And what next? Don't we need two of them? Most of my nurses have two ears". After that bit of humor, he was delighted at the laughter of his friends who were crowding nearby to see what he had made.

I explained that we would have to let it dry out, and then sand it to remove all rough edges and then fire it in the ceramic kiln and that it would be ready for him to paint the next week. We started the procedure with the ball of clay again and Tony labored and labored with his one moveable thumb. Bob lay nearby with an expression on his face like a father watching his son knock a home run at the ballpark.

Just as we finished cleaning bits of dust and clay from Tony, Bob called out, "Tony's a dirt-dauber now.!" This caused a burst of laughter from the crowd. I quickly stuck my hand in some liquid clay and smeared it on Tony's face and on his little hand.

His happy eyes met mine. "Thanks, Dottie,. I never got dirty before." I hugged him very carefully, knowing how fragile his little body was. Those who could, clapped their hands and gave him a big cheer.

My phone was ringing when I got home from work that night. It was Bob, and he wanted to talk about Little Tony.

"What a spunky little guy that Tony is," were the openers. He went on to tell me that he had learned a big lesson tonight. "I learned that we should not look at people to see what they can't do, but we should keep our eyes on what they can do with what they have."

His profound remark left me stunned and I waited to hear what he would say next. He finally asked if I really thought Tony would be able to paint the earrings.

"I really think so, Bob. He can move his head almost two inches so I am pretty certain he can paint them if he wants to."

"This I've got to see. Gee," he went on thoughtfully, "and I thought I was in bad shape, not being able to use my fingers and only able to life my forearms elbow high. Wow!"

The week passed quickly and Tony was eager to see his little leaves. We had the paint and brush ready for him when they brought him. I asked if he thought he could hold the brush between his teeth, and if he could, we would dip the brush in the paint and with the two-inch movement of his head he would be able to accomplish the job.

"I'm ready, if you are," he answered. Bob gave Tony an admiring smile and a big wink when we held the little leaf on a saucer under his chin and placed the brush, wet with paint, in Tony's mouth. He gripped it with his teeth and went to work, slowly moving his head back and forth. He rested a few minutes, surveying the results. His friends gave him another big cheer when he had finished with the second one. I explained that we would have them fired and ready for him the following week. He wondered aloud how the pink glaze he had painted on them could possibly turn green in the kiln. He enjoyed the teasing his friends gave him about painting his leaves pink.

In all, it took Tony six pain-staking weeks to make six pair of earrings. This held a sense of accomplishment for Tony that he had never known.

One of our faithful volunteers went to a craft shop and bought the backings and while shopping, purchased some tiny white gift boxes. We placed his first pair of earrings in the box. They looked like little green gems lying on their soft bed of white cotton. After looking at them, Tony raised his eyes proudly to see if his friends saw what he had made. He was ecstatic.

Before he left to go home, we tucked the little box in his shirt pocket just under his chin. When anyone asked him about his earrings he would urge him or her to look at the pair in his pocket.

The ambulance from the County Home and Hospital arrived one half hour early the next week. I watched them enter the gate and back up to the ramp at the big double door. I saw the driver get out and walk to the back of the vehicle and open the ambulance door. To my surprise, he didn't take Little Tony out but instead walked into the building and to my office window. When he was sure he had my attention he called through to me, "Tony wants you to come to him, right away."

My heart was in my throat as I envisioned that Tony had been hurt. We had been cautioned that he must never be moved inside his bed and also never be bumped or jarred. I envisioned the worst and ran as fast as I could to check out the situation. I climbed up in the ambulance and looked at Little Tony. I could see at first glance that he was grinning from ear to ear. I breathed a sigh of relief as I went to his side.

"Look in my shirt pocket, Dottie," he quickly said, his eyes never leaving my face; what I saw there was indeed a surprise. There was a bunch of bills rolled loosely together, with the tops sticking out of his pocket so that Tony could see it from the position of his head.

"My gosh, Tony, what did you do…rob a bank?" I asked.

Tony let out a big laugh. "No," he quickly answered. "I sold my earrings! Yep," he said proudly, "I tried to give them to the nurses but they wouldn't accept them as gifts. But they really wanted them to remember me by so they bought them. They paid me two dollars a pair. I didn't need their money as I get everything I need or want at the home, but they insisted." I slowly counted out the 12 one-dollar bills with Tony watching intently.

"Why Tony, that's wonderful. Now would you like me to go shopping for you?"

"No, Dottie. This is the first money I ever earned in my life and I want you to buy something for the club, or give it to some member who needs it. You see," he went on, "I have never been able to give anyone a gift, especially something that I made by myself. When it comes to gifts, it seems I have always been on the receiving end."

It was as if a magnet was holding our eyes together. Suddenly, Tony broke the silence, "Why Dottie you're crying!"

"I can't help it, Tony," I sobbed. I tried to find a safe way to hug him. I gave him a kiss on his brow and whispered in his ear, "I love you, Tony." I saw a tear slip out of his eye and ooze slowly down the side of his face and settle in his big smile.

"Hey, Guy," I mumbled, "I've got to go to work." I backed out of the ambulance and walked quickly inside the building, wiping my eyes. I was silently praying, "Thank you God for this moment and thank you for Little Tony."

It was only a few weeks later when Tony's father appeared at the County Home and Hospital, searching for his son. The authorities had to first consider how this tremendous shock would affect Little Tony's heart condition. Counseling was recommended by the doctor as the appropriate way to handle it. They felt Tony's father also needed some preparation for the belated meeting. They found him willing to do anything just to get to spend some time with his only son again.

Mr. Gonzales was later offered a paid position with the hospital to be Little Tony's twenty-four hour a day aide. He was happy about this arrangement as he had no wife to go home to. He told Tony that she had died of a broken heart shortly after they had left him at the Home and Hospital.

Tony attended the next meeting beaming with pride as he introduced the man in white, at his side, as his father. Each of the members took turns going over to them and expressing their love and admiration for his son and welcoming him home. A big smile never left this father's face the entire evening and he was awestruck with the acceptance and love everyone had for his son. He told us that he intended to come to all the meetings from then on.

Bob called as soon as he got home to expound about the marvelous job Tony had done on his earrings.. "Gee, if he can do that with one moveable thumb and a two-inch movement of his head, I should be able to do something too, After all, I can move both of my arms up to the elbows."

I assured him that we would have a project for him to do the next week.

The following week, Gladys went back and searched through her shop and came across four coffee cups all baked and ready for glazing.

After Bob had said hello to everyone that night, he asked to be moved to the ceramic class. We had the tape ready and set about securing the paintbrush to his hand. With the forward movement of his arm he was able to dip the brush into the little jar of white glaze and sling it awkwardly toward the first cup. We laughed when we saw as much glaze on the tray as was on the cup. It took him all evening to complete the four cups but he was very satisfied with his efforts. Tony called him a speed demon for painting so fast…four cups in one night but at the same time, teased him about wasting so much of the glaze.

When Bob returned the next week, his cups, shiny bright, were on display in the center of the ceramic table. All of his friends took turns looking at them and complimenting Bob on a job well done. He beamed as he watched us pack them into a shoebox all stuffed with tissue paper to take to his mother.

8

They wheeled Bob up the ramp and into the building. He was sitting in a wheelchair, wearing a bright red shirt, loose-fitting trousers (to hide the bag strapped to his leg) and shoes. He came in his chair only on special occasions; although he never felt discomfort from it, his body often reacted and gave him problems afterwards. Besides, it was always easier for him to come on his stretcher.

"Hey man," someone called out to him. "Why so dressed up? Getting married or something?"

He shot him a big grin and answered, "No, but we have a big meeting tonight."

You could have heard a pin drop, when he later called the meeting to order. Jan sat at his side with pad and pen to record the minutes of this important occasion.

After the reading of the minutes of the last meeting, he called out in his biggest voice, "Any new business?"

It was obvious that the meeting had been preplanned when hands shot up all over the room. Ronnie Richardson, a young man of slight build who had wrapped his car around a telephone pole on graduation night, resulting in paralysis of his lower limbs, pulled his chair forward before starting his speech.

"Mr. President," he began. "We're ready for some action!"

I sat there stunned, waiting for his next words.

The Dear Frances Letter

"We have enjoyed the club activities but a bunch of us are getting bored. I'm afraid we are going to lose some of our good members if we don't do something about it."

Bob interrupted in a stern voice, disapprovingly, "And what do you have in mind, Ronnie?"

"Well, I've been reading about a wheelchair basketball team in California, sponsored by the Easter Seal Agency. Why can't we have basketball too? We have the courts right outside. Many of us paraplegics shoot baskets to get our daily exercise. Shooting baskets is wonderful therapy to strengthen our upper bodies. Sure would be nice to play some real basketball and have some competition among us."

Excitement was written all over Bob's face when he asked for my thoughts on the subject. There were many loud "Yeas" coming from the men in the room.

"I say let's do it!" I answered quickly amid the boisterous reaction in the room.

Bob was grinning like the proverbial cat that swallowed the canary when he called the meeting back to order.

"Okay, Ronnie," he said in the best business voice he could muster, "I appoint you as chairman of a committee of your choice, to send away for the rules and regulations of wheelchair basketball so we can do this thing right."

"Any further business?" No answers from the group. "This meeting is adjourned."

Total success and happiness shone from Bob's face when he said goodbye to his friends that night with most of them commenting on how well he had conducted the meeting.

Bob was thrilled to receive a call during the week from the Superintendent of Recreation. She asked if he would mind calling a special meeting of the men wishing to play basketball so she could meet them in person. As usual, Bob, in his most gracious manner, welcomed her heartily.

Telephones buzzed all over the city after this great piece of news. Many of the men came early to the meeting to insure that they heard every word.

Mrs. Cordelia Hunt, better known as Dee Dee to her friends and employees in the recreation department, was ready for them. She was impressed with Bob's introduction and more than a little surprised and somewhat tickled, when at one point he referred to her by her nickname. She had brought with her two new basketballs and two new nets. But the biggest surprise of all was when she introduced the handsome young man at her side as Chuck Wilson, their new coach. The applause was almost deafening. Many of the men reared up on their wheels to show their prowess.

Before she left, Dee Dee asked if she might have a few private minutes with Bob and me. She immediately started maneuvering Bob's wheelchair through the crowd, toward my little office. Bob rode sitting tall and still with all the aplomb of a newly appointed knight, eyes staring straight ahead. When she attempted to turn the sharp narrow corner to enter the office door, she was horrified by a loud bump.

"Oh my," she cried out in horror. Did I hurt you?"

Bob let out one of his quick belly laughs, "I wish! Just don't hit me on my head. That's the only place I have feelings."

Mrs. Hunt, formally an army Colonel, attempting to regain her composure, said in her best military voice, "I am very impressed with you, Bob, and I would like to ask you a couple of personal questions."

Bob met her eyes, unabashed, and said, "Okay, shoot."

"I have heard that you do a great job counseling some of the members. Would you share with me what you would say to someone who recently had a serious accident and became paralyzed?"

Bob smiled at her and said in a soft voice,"Simple. I'd just tell them to keep on going and be all that they can be. They got to live till they die."

"That's wonderful advice, Bob. But were you always able to live by that philosophy?"

Bob's face became serious and thoughtful. "Well, no, not really. It took me some time to realize that I couldn't take a handful of pills 'cause my hands don't work. And, I couldn't confront a telephone pole with my car, 'cause I can't drive. And I couldn't hold a gun to my head. I finally came to the conclusion that I had no choice but to keep on going, be the best that I can be and LIVE until I die."

"Thanks Bob. I'm going to remember that."

All eyes were on Bob when he returned to the auditorium, feeling ten feet tall.

The men took this wheelchair basketball seriously and practiced every available minute. They learned to pull twice on their wheel and then bounce the ball on the court, constituting a dribble. It didn't take long for Coach Chuck to see why the rule of personal foul had been included, as some, in their eagerness, would grab their opponent's wheel to slow them down or interrupt a fast shot at the net. Crowds of interested citizens lined the sidelines each evening and watched with amazement at the dexterity and skills of the team. Bob was usually among the spectators cheering them on. He said he watched them to get some exercise for himself.

It wasn't long before the men began to hunger for an opposing team to compete with, but at that time to our knowledge, there was no other wheelchair basketball team in the southeastern part of the United States. Soon, the idea was born to challenge the men in the North Tampa Chamber of Commerce (in wheel chairs, of course), to a regulation game and at the same time, stage a money-raising community dinner to raise funds for securing matching red jerseys for the team. The adult advisory council for the center volunteered to prepare the dinner for them. The teen club members volunteered to sell tickets.

The publicity for this event was awesome, with coverage by all the local media and then later on by the Associated Press. This Associated Press item caught the attention of one of the larger wheel-chair manufacturers. They contacted us the next week with a request that one of our skilled players be sent to Atlanta, all expenses paid, to give a demonstration to their employees.

Bob called another special meeting and asked for a vote on which player should be allowed to go. Ronnie Richardson, a speed demon on the court and having the eye of an eagle for the basket, was voted in unanimously. Despite the Tampa Rockets staking the men from the chamber thirty points at the beginning of the game due to their inexperience, the Rockets won by an embarrassing score. Bob gave a short speech at the end of the game, thanking the Chamber of Commerce Members for their support, with tongue in cheek, consoled them by telling them that they were pretty good, but just needed more experience."

~The Wheelchair Basketball Team in Tampa, Florida~

He was heard to tell the Mayor at half time, while staring at the chamber men panting on the sidelines and the Mayor's graying hair, "This is not exactly a fair game. We had you beat before we started with our age and experience." The Mayor agreed, walking away to conceal his merriment.

Bob, in his usual encouraging way, urged Ronnie on and all but held his breath until he returned from Atlanta.

The wheelchair company, being very impressed with Ronnie's demonstration, offered a one-year contract, with a small salary and all expenses, plus a new chair for each man on the team to tour the United States and Canada to demonstrate the strength and dexterity of their brand of chairs.

The men's excitement was equaled only by Bob's enthusiasm. He opened most of his business meetings thereafter by giving a full report on the men's travels and progress, having phoned family members for updates. He dubbed his favorite players as: White Lightening, The Rocket, The Beaver, The Eagle Eye and lastly the The Bomb. The Bomb acquired his new title because of his unusually broad shoulders and strength. Great though his skills were, he was a terror when he barreled down the court, sometimes creating havoc when he reached out to grab his opponent's brakes.

When the men returned after a year of exciting travels and fun, most enrolled in special courses or went out and sought, with great success, permanent employment. Some took brush-up courses on knowledge they had gained earlier but had never put to real use. Some had to limit their attendance to the club activities as they were pretty busy with their own affairs.

9

After many months of studying and cramming, the time came for Bob to take his final insurance test.

The instructor told him in advance that no one was to be allowed in the room while he took the test. Bob explained to him how we had studied together and he would feel better if I could be in the room with him. This was a "No-go" from the outset and Bob took a personal dislike for the instructor from that moment on.

I paced the floor at my home all the next day, waiting for the results of the test. My phone never rang.

When I could stand it no more, I called his home. His mother answered and was crying so hard I could hardly understand her. I guessed that Bob had failed the test but I could not imagine how.

"It's okay, Mrs. Baker," I found myself saying. "Bob can take the test over again. Many people don't pass the first time around and some have to take it several times before passing it."

"But, you don't understand," she sobbed. "He didn't even take the test."

"What do you mean he didn't take the test?" I screamed into the phone.

"He just got mad at the instructor and refused to take it."

I recall slamming the phone down and rushing to my car. Luck was with me as I drove like a mad person to Bob's house. His mother was leaning against the front door as I swished by her rushing to Bob's room.

He looked shyly at me, trying to muster a smile, but it just made him look more ill at ease. Finally, I broke the silence that hung like a wet blanket between us, "What in the world happened to you, Bob?" I scolded.

"Give me a chance to explain, Dottie, please." he begged. I just stared at him and found no words to express the let down that I felt. Disappointment rushed through my veins like a raging river and I knew I had better leave before I said things I might regret later. I left the room with no further comment.

Three days passed. Bob called each day and when I heard his voice, I hung up. His mother called on the fourth day.

"We have got to talk, Dottie," she pleaded. "I don't blame you for being mad at Bob. I am too. But it has made him sick. He is refusing to eat or drink anything and in his condition, this can be very serious. If he doesn't take in enough liquids his kidney will go bad and he has only one left. You wouldn't believe how small his urine output is. Please Dottie, you just have to come talk with him. I can't do a thing with him."

I had been in their home enough to know about the problems Bob had with his one remaining kidney. His mother was constantly pushing water and juices down him and I would be asked to leave the room frequently while she took care of his urine bag. There were always two or three glasses of liquid on his bedside table. I thought back on how he taught me how to place the rim of the glass on his bottom lip, allowing him to tip it with an upward movement of his arm and hand, as much as was needed to control the quantity.

I heard his mother's voice droning on the phone. "Would you please come talk to him just for me?" she pleaded.

"I shouldn't, but I will," I finally conceded, realizing that she was hurting, maybe even worse than I was.

Once again I drove as fast as I dared and Bob's mother met me at the door. I walked by her with only a nod of recognition. He didn't raise his eyes to meet mine as was usually his habit, and no smile was evident on his face. His eyes were encircled with black like someone had used mascara around them.

"How dare you," I yelled at him, as my anger at him had increased with each mile. "You knew every bit of that information," I sobbed. "You never missed one question on that practice test and you almost knew the answers verbatim. What on earth were you thinking that you didn't take the test? I will never forgive you for this. You have wasted time all these months. You have no regard for yourself, your mother, your friends and none for me either. I am through playing games with you. You have let us all down."

My knees were shaking when I stood to leave.

"Please Dottie, let me explain. I am truly ashamed. I am sorry I let you down, but…"

"Don't give me any 'BUTS'. There is no excuse for what you have done." I sank wearily into the familiar chair by his bed and I could no longer hold back my tears.

Tears were streaming down his face. He searched my face with pleading eyes.

"It is inexcusable. I have wasted my time with you. You don't care about anyone but yourself," I went on. From now on, you can get yourself another playmate, one who doesn't mind wasting time with a quitter. I have more important things to do."

I rose to my feet with knees shaking and turned to go. I heard a loud sob.

"Let me tell you just how it was. I was afraid. I was afraid I would fail the test. My life has been one big failure after another. Nothing works out for me. Can you understand?"

"Indeed I do not understand" I retorted. "You had to know that you could pass that test. Think of all the reviewing we did and you knew all the answers."

"I know, I know," he agreed. "But you don't know how scared I was. Things have been going so well and I couldn't take the chance of messing up again."

"Aw, grow up, Bob," I scolded. "Don't you know that to try even if you fail, is honorable? But, to fail because you were afraid to try is nothing short of being plain dishonorable."

I couldn't meet his mother's tear-filled eyes as I rushed by her. All I wanted at that moment was the feel of my husband Ray's strong arms around me. Only he could help me through this.

I explained that I was not coming back and that I was thoroughly disgusted with Bob. "I have more important things to do."

As I was leaving, my thoughts went back to the many times I had attempted to give him something to drink only to find how difficult it was with him lying face down. I couldn't hold back a smile when I recalled the first time I had offered to feed him his lunch.

I remembered Bob saying to me, "Can't you just say 'help me with my lunch'? Sounds a lot better to my ears than 'can I feed you?' The latter reminds me of someone feeding a pig." Another lesson learned, I had thought at the time, cringing from his scolding.

Slowly, I relented, retracing my steps to the back bedroom. I knew I could not desert him now. Our lives had become too entwined. Suddenly, I realized that Bob had been like a little boy seeing his shadow for the first time. He had been honest with me and had been truly afraid to take the test. Bob's mother entered the room, bringing two big bowls of chicken soup.

"May I help you with your lunch," I asked. He readily agreed with his eyes smiling at me. Both bowls were empty in no time flat with Bob asking for a refill.

Then we plotted our strategy on how to best approach the instructor at Rehab, and to convince him to give Bob a second chance. Since the truth is always the best, I suggested to Bob that he just tell the man the truth.

Bob called Rehab the next day and arrangements were made as to the date and time when he would take the test. He and his mother spent the next two weeks reviewing his books and cramming for the test. He was not only ready to take the test but also eager to get at it. The instructor shared Bob's pride when Bob made one of the highest grades possible.

10

Bob made his own arrangements with his friend at the funeral home to transport him one day a week to Lester's office to do his internship.

The first visible sign of progress that I saw in Bob after his first session with Les was a writing pen taped to the palm of his hand. His mother had wound narrow tape around the end of the pen making a soft ball. With the telephone receiver anchored around his neck and this contraption on his hand, he discovered that he could use the phone without assistance. Another door seemed to have opened for him. He spent hours on end contacting his friends to let them know he was officially in business. He had business cards printed, and a large white sign with BIG, black letters showing his name and business, soon hung from an ornamental post in his front yard.

Most of his friends at the Center, upon hearing that Bob was ready to open his own agency, cancelled their insurance and purchased new policies from him. Many of the workers at the recreation department followed suit. My husband insured his company's delivery trucks and salesmen's cars, and our private cars with Baker Insurance.

His neighbors and his mailman dropped by to congratulate him and, while there, were so impressed with Bob's accomplishments that many chose to change their policies. In only a short time, the secretary had almost more work than she could keep up with. He soon hired another lady who was more experienced in writing policies.

Bob decided he had to figure a better way to connect his bedroom to his office. After consulting with the telephone company a rotary system was installed.

When his bank account could afford it, Bob advertised in the paper for nurses. He became proficient in handling and scheduling their work shifts. The nurse prepared his meals as well as took care of his personal needs. His mother could most often be found in one of the many flowerbeds, setting out new plants, weeding or watering them. She was enjoying her newfound freedom and became her jovial self again.

One day, after finishing his breakfast, the nurse folded the *Tribune* to the Real Estate section and placed it on his table in front of him. Bob loved to browse through the For Sale section. He let out a yell that brought the nurse running quickly back to his side.

"Look at that," he yelled, while pointing the pen strapped on his hand at the paper. She leaned over him to read the item of interest. Due to widening of a street in Ybor City, a family was offering a brick home for sale, cheap. It had to be moved off the property. Bob called the owner and asked that he come to his office with pictures of the house.

Bob said he had to do a lot of wheeling and dealing before the owner accepted his offer but the deal was finally made. After that was the process of contacting his accountant and his banker and getting the house moved. They already owned a corner lot behind his mother's house. He had no trouble making all the tough business arrangements but the big decision of which street should the house face? - almost stumped him.

His mother chose one street and Bob chose another. Since it was a corner lot, they had a choice and it took days for them to come to an agreement about which one would be best for the front of the house. Bob finally won the argument: they decided to put the office facing the side street and the front of the house on the busier street. Bob wanted to make certain his clients could get in and out of his four-car parking lot when they came to do business with him.

~Bob shortly after moving into his new home~

Days and weeks passed with Bob watching the remodeling of his new brick home through his window. He became so absorbed in it that the girls in the office teased him about the need for them to hire a new boss. Bob accepted their teasing in good nature and everybody took turns watching as his dream was coming true right before their eyes

Bob sits in his wheel chair in front of the big glass window he was so proud of. For years, he had not seen the dawn of day, nor experienced the warm sunshine on his face in the afternoons.

When the movers had the house all back together again, Bob added a large, long bedroom for himself, where a porch had been removed. French doors divided his bedroom from his spacious new office, which was about twelve feet from his bedroom. Behind his bedroom, a door opened into the main part of the new house consisting of a small room which his mother would use as her bedroom in order to be near to him, three full sized bedrooms, dining room, living room and baths. The kitchen was small but near enough that Bob could smell the nice aromas coming from it when he was in bed. He grew to like that a lot.

The plants that had surrounded the house before it was moved were part of the house deal and Bob and his mother arranged for their gardener to move them to their new yard. Soon the big brick home looked as if it had been there forever. His mother was proudest of the four-foot tall azaleas that they planted around the base of the house, making it look as if it had always stood there.

The nurse put Bob in his wheelchair and he was given a tour of the interior of the house. He remained silent, with a broad smile covering his face throughout the tour. When it was finished they pushed him to the front door of his new office. While sitting outside at the foot of the concrete steps, Bob stated: "I have heard it said that God never closes a door without opening a window for us. Well, he sure is opening a lot of windows for me."

His nurse pushed Bob on around the exterior of the house, passing his office windows and stopped in front of the windows looking into his bedroom. He was still beaming with pleasure when she pushed him up the ramp leading to a covered walkway and through the door that opened into his empty bedroom. Once there, he let out a whoop. "Wow! What a big room!"

After he looked out the window, he let his eyes roam around the room, saying, "Funny part of it is, in my dreams my new home was always going to be red brick and yet here it is cream-colored brick. Think the old man upstairs pulled a joke on me? He probably thought I had been too choosy!" He was laughing at his own joke.

The nurse and his mother pushed Bob in his chair back out of the house and down the street to their old, small frame house. They prepared him for bed, shortly afterwards and he found sleep impossible. He kept going over and over the many things that had been happening in his life. It was too good to be true.

11

When my phone rang the next morning, I knew it would be Bob. And it was. But, the message he had for me was not what I expected. He wanted me to come over at once, or at least as soon as possible.

His mother met me at the door with a big smile on her face, so I knew everything was all right.

"Bob called me to come over at once," I said to her. "What's up?"

"Come on in. He has some great news for you." We walked rapidly back to Bob's room and Bob was aglow with happiness.

"You'll never guess what has happened!" he exclaimed breathlessly. "I won the lottery!"

"What do you mean?" I asked, catching the excitement.

"I won six thousand, five hundred dollars."

"You did what?" I asked in surprise.

"I forgot to tell you that I give one of my nurses one dollar a week to buy a ticket for me and it has finally paid off!"

"Wow, Bob, that's wonderful."

He went on, "And now I have to decide what to do with it." His mother was laughing too.

"What do you suggest, Dottie?"

My eyes looked around the room to take inventory of potential needs, and before I knew it, I spoke out hurriedly," Maybe you can knock out that wall with the two regular windows and replace it with a large plate glass window so you can see the sun come up in the mornings. I remember on my first visit with you, when you said you wanted a view that would enable you to see the sun come up or the sun set. Maybe this is your chance to get that."

Bob turned real serious and for a moment, I wondered if I had spoken too soon.

"Hum, that's a great idea" he said, breaking the silence while staring at the small windows and the long wall. His mother chimed in with "Gee, that would be great."

We sat together talking about Bob's good luck.

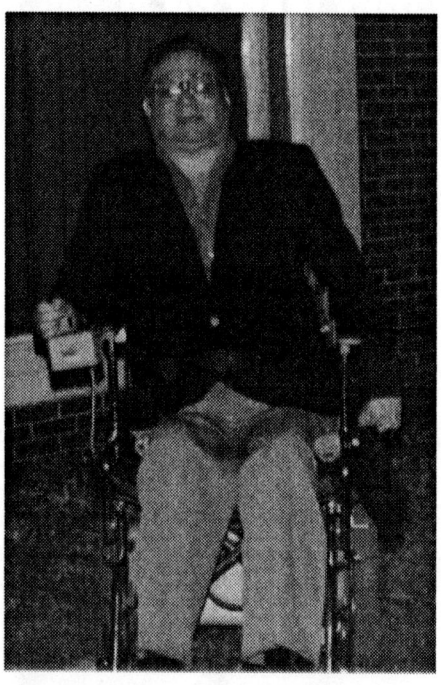

~Bob in front of his beautiful new plate-glass window~

The Dear Frances Letter

"Seriously, I don't think it was luck at all. I think it was my Friend upstairs showering me with more gifts. All these good things that are happening in my life have to come from somewhere, and it certainly isn't coming from me."

I looked at him long and hard and after much thought, I finally said, "I don't know about that, Bob. Sometimes, I don't think you are aware of the influence you have on people. It is pretty obvious to me that you are spending most of your time doing and thinking of things you can do for those less fortunate than you."

He gave me a grateful smile as I was leaving and urged me to come back soon. He had a smug look on his face.

Although we talked daily, there was no further mention of his great winnings and I had just about forgotten about it. But, one day, he insisted that I come over as he had a surprise for me. I tried to wheedle it out of him, but to no avail. I saw the surprise when I was approaching his house. A large picture window, from ceiling to a foot above the floor, had been placed in his eastern wall. Bob was sitting outside in his yard in front of his beautiful window. He was all dressed up in his Dad's blue sports jacket and dress trousers, with a camera lying on the chair beside him. He wanted his picture taken right then and there.

When we went inside his room, his mother had made refreshments and we had a big celebration with good treats and lots of laughter.

He met new people almost every night when he went to the club. He always followed up the next day with a personal phone call to get better acquainted. More often than not, he would sell them an insurance policy while they were talking. He had developed a wonderful soft-sell manner, which he always denied. Nevertheless, a lot of insurance policies were sold while he was making many new friends.

He started inviting some of them over to play cards in the evenings. With his mother holding his cards, he became adept at pointing with the pencil strapped on his right hand at the card he wanted her to play. To his delight, they won so often that he was almost ashamed to check with the scorekeeper. He sometimes kept a running score in his mind. He discovered that his concentration was improving and he dearly loved the games. But most of all, he enjoyed visiting with his friends and rapping with them when the game was over. He seldom ate the cookies and colas that his mother served as he was still self-conscience about needing assistance with such a simple matter as eating.

12

The doctor was appalled with the condition of Bob's body when he came by for his monthly checkup. He shook his head in dismay each time he discovered a new hot spot and saw the many red areas that had appeared since his last visit. He told Bob he would send someone out from an orthopedic company to look at them and recommend which way they should go from there. They had to make some changes if he was going to continue working in his office.

The orthopedic specialist said that Bob could no longer stay such long hours on his back or on his tummy. His tissues were breaking down. He recommended that he start using a hoist with custom made braces to fit the weight bearing parts of his body. The hoist would make it easier for the nurses to lift and swing him from one position to another. Bob was terrified. He wondered how he could continue to work each day from such a contraption. He could not imagine doing business while hanging from the tall metal frame that supported the hoist. It took more than a little persuasion for Bob to consent to give it a try.

"But you do what you have to do in this life" he muttered to no one in particular. "It looks like a giant grasshopper. Damn!"

It didn't take long for Bob to realize, however, that the sling was just what he needed. I suspect that it took us longer to get used to seeing him hanging in the air. The custom-made body brace repositioned him in such a way that it took care of all the hot spots on his body and his general health improved in no time. The Orthopedic Technician had even constructed a small desk for his telephone and a place for his paper work. This made it possible for him to function more efficiently as well as to be more independent.

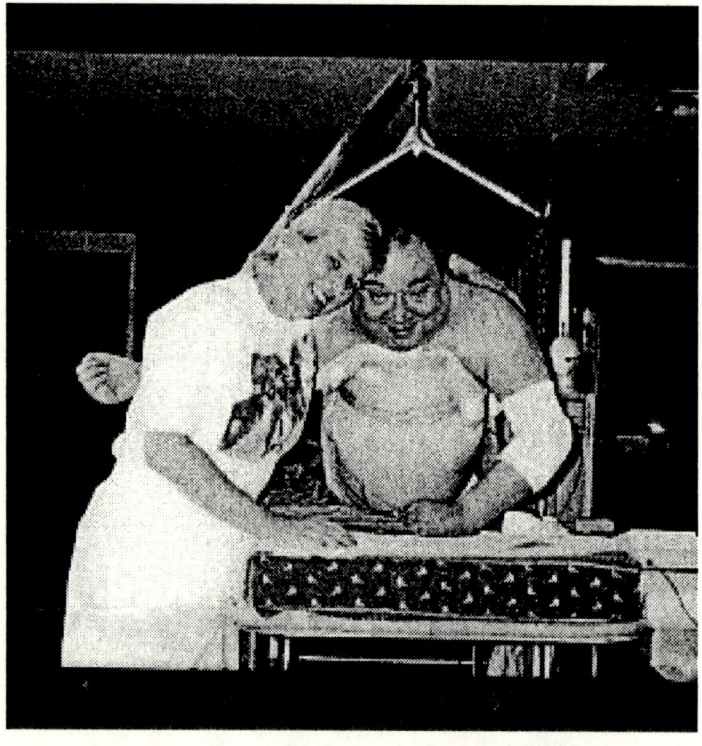

~Longtime friend Sherry Dulworth with Bob~

An ambitious young reporter named Jerald Hyche who worked for *The Tampa Tribune* heard about Bob's accomplishments and called to make an appointment to interview him. Bob was ecstatic but rather shy when the time for the interview came. Finally, he opened up to the reporter and in no time he had made a new friend.

The article would be about three quadriplegics in the business world who were successful despite their physical limitations. He didn't much like the idea of his picture being in the paper, but the reporter convinced him it would be good for his business. Bob conceded. To his utter amazement, in the *Baylife* section of *The Tampa Tribune*'s Sunday paper was a large picture of Bob lying on his stomach on a stretcher and conducting business in his office. Les was in the picture also, with a picture of Joe Sanchez, another Quadriplegic whom Bob had helped to get started in the insurance business, sitting in his wheelchair at his desk in his office. Friends from all over the city called to congratulate him. It surprised Bob that many of his clients hadn't known that he was paralyzed until the write-up in the paper. Bob had been referred to them as the most honest and reliable man in town to do business with.

~

It was in late summer and the sun was shining brightly into the office window and into Bob's eyes. For the second time he had asked the secretary to close the blinds a little more. "Why won't you let me shut the blinds all the way, Bob?" she asked.

"No," he answered abruptly. "I like to see who is coming." He told her he had been giving it some thought on how to keep the sun from shining in his eyes, and he'd have a solution to that problem soon. Within the week a large delivery truck backed into Bob's driveway loaded with a big tree. He had ordered a fifteen-foot tall, ten-foot wide Florida Orchid Tree. He could hardly lie still as he watched the men plant it. It was beautiful! When the men had finished planting it, it looked as if it had grown from infancy in that very same location.

My call from Bob that night was a memorable one, with our conversation dealing with one subject, Bob's tree. The girls in the office kidded Bob about baby-sitting his tree and being afraid to go to bed lest someone come in and steal it.

He smiled throughout their teasing and rather enjoyed it and the excitement his tree created in the neighborhood. He drew such pleasure from it that he ordered another one the next week and had it planted outside his picture window, partially blocking his view of the alley. "I'm the last of the "big spenders"" he laughingly told me.

13

A skinny black and white cat showed up every day just outside Bob's window. While looking at it one day, he told the nurse to feed that poor hungry cat, as he didn't like to think of anything, especially a poor helpless cat that looked very much like one they used to have when he was a kid, being hungry. The cat returned every day to Bob's delight to get her handout. After a few weeks, it was evident that she was going to have kittens so Bob insisted the nurse increase her food.

A short while later, the nurse walked in Bob's room holding an arm full of baby kittens. He immediately chose the one that most closely resembled his childhood memory and named it "Shogun."

After that, it became a daily routine for the nurse to bring Shogun in from the garage to visit his master. At first they placed the baby kitten on Bob's bare back. Later Bob asked that they put it around his neck so that he could feel it. The nurse swore that the cat sensed Bob's predicament and enjoyed its visit as much as Bob did.

~

In looking through his mail in January of 1979, Bob's secretary had opened and placed in front of him a letter from Exchange Bancorporation, Inc. The President

Dorothy Brosch

of the bank, William C. MacInnes, had been elected to chair a committee to establish a Comprehensive Physical Rehabilitation Center on the grounds at Tampa General Hospital and he would be interested in having Bob serve on the steering committee. He would notify him at a later date as to time and place of the meeting. Bob dictated a reply to his secretary, giving a resounding "Yes."

The first meeting was held in the bank. Bob attended, and having outgrown his one and only suit, he went dressed in his father's only suit. His mother had had an awful time at the Goodwill store, finding a pair of shoes that they could get his curled toes and feet into. She had borrowed several pairs to try on him at home. The solution to the shoe problem came when they discovered he would need a much larger size and they could stuff the toes of the shoes with tissue paper to make them fit. For once in his life, Bob was glad he didn't have to walk and could ride in his chair.

> *For all that work (very little of it was the result of my efforts) we now have a very large and highly respected rehabilitation center adjacent to TGH. I was finally able to go through the center in 1987. They were not able to do much for me, but it was most gratifying to see such a magnificent facility for helping people with all types of medical problems needing rehabilitation. There is even a heliport so that severely injured people can be brought right to the very entrance.*

He enjoyed the meeting. He was introduced and treated like a VIP but admitted later that he felt he didn't contribute much to the discussion. He watched avidly for letters to arrive from the president of the bank, keeping him informed about their progress and he answered each one making his own suggestions. Several years later, Bob was taken to see the Rehabilitation

Center in its completed form. At the hospital, he was very excited over the helipad on top of the building. He was grinning when he told the chairman of the project that it was too late to help him in any way, but he sure was proud to know that others who needed help would be able to get it right here, in our city.

~

During the 1970's, I was involved in local politics in a minor way. As you can see by the enclosed letters, my involvement was very small, but most enlightening! My work with the Hillsboro {sic} County Democratic Committee was mostly "smoke filled room" type stuff and not very exciting. However, work with the steering committee was truly gratifying. Mr. William McInnes was the President of the Exchange Bank and President of Tampa Electric Company at that time and he was a real trip to work with – in most ways he acted just like an ordinary working man. However he was a very powerful man and clearly meant business!

It was only a matter of weeks before Bob found among his many pieces of mail a letter from the Democratic Executive Committee of Florida requesting his assistance in the upcoming election. It suddenly dawned on him that he had never registered to vote in all these years and he felt deeply honored by this letter. He called the Voter Registration Bureau and requested a form be sent to his home. He registered as a Republican, though, because of his admiration of Ronald Reagan. It spurred him into wondering just how many of the Club members had never registered nor voted.

A swift call to the Voters Registration Bureau produced much interest and they lost no time, with Bob's help, in registering as many from the Center as were interested. From that time on, the word spread that Bob was more than a little bit interested in politics and he became a target for candidates seeking his vote. For a while he became greatly interested in politics and considered each of their visits a great honor, plus he learned more and more about the local and national political scene. People who talked with Bob were often amazed at how he stayed abreast of the city's development and how well informed he was about the various candidates who were running for public office.

He had much to share with Jan and the crowd at the Monday night programs. He would collect their thoughts and when he felt they would be of interest to the Committee, he would rush another letter to the Chairman with his report.

14

Jan invited one of her friends that she had met while going to business school to attend a Monday night meeting with her. When she introduced Bunny to Bob, she noticed an instant attraction between them. Bob asked someone standing nearby to write her name and phone number on a scrap of paper and put it in his breast pocket.

The next day, he called her and during a lengthy exchange she told him she had Lupus disease and didn't have long to live, according to doctor's reports. He explained his condition to her and they both had laughed, saying at least they had one thing in common. They both were going to die sooner than later. As the friendship grew, their bond became stronger by the day. Soon Bob had a confidant that he could share his innermost thoughts with. It wasn't long before she would pay him regular visits. Many times she encouraged her mother to go along with her so they could get into a challenging card game with both of their mothers.

Unfortunately, Bunny succumbed to her disease all too soon, giving Bob his first brush with losing a loved one. It was a tough pill for him to swallow but he finally accepted the finality of it and lost himself in his business at hand. Jan and other friends encouraged him along the way with their almost daily phone calls and weekly visits but it was obvious that Bob would have to work his way through this devastating loss, in his own way and in his own time.

The Dear Frances Letter

His pals at the club threw a big birthday bash at his home for him when he turned 40. It was an "open house" party, as his office wouldn't accommodate all the wheelchairs at the same time. He couldn't believe how his office staff and friends had pulled such a surprise on him. His amazement grew at each new arrival but he had a new quip or joke for each one. The table laden with snacks and foods had been sneaked in behind his back.

Bob laughed with the male guests and flirted with all the ladies. I suspected that he still thought of himself as the handsome young man in boxer shorts, in the picture hanging prominently on his wall. But in truth, his appearance seemed to be changing rapidly. In addition to gaining weight from an insatiable appetite, some of the many medications he had to take daily were causing him to retain fluids. It was hard to tell where his head ended and his neck began. His receding hairline only accented his fat cheeks and big blue eyes, making him look all the more like a chubby little boy peeping out of a big motionless body of a fully-grown man.

When the last guest had left, Bob said he was starving and in between bites that his nurse fed him, he was talking about his wonderful friends. The fact that Jan had come to his party with a couple of other paraplegics didn't bother him at all. His mad love for her had long since cooled, leaving them the very best of friends. He was delighted to see her so happy. She had already warned him that she was seeing one of them quite regularly. Bob was thrilled for her and hoped her new relationship would be a lasting one.

15

As the years passed, Bob's business grew ever larger and more time consuming. Under the guidance of his good friend and mentor, Les, he opened a second office in the southern part of the county. He was able to hire a man and his wife who had been operating a small insurance office in the area to manage his branch office. When his main office in his home became inundated with paper work, he would transfer part of the overload to the branch office. This proved to be a promising addition to his business and in no time sales had increased and it proved to be a lucrative venture.

Bob's friend, Stuart Kah, dropped in to see him one day. He had been out looking for a job. "No one wants to hire a man who can't walk and is dependent on a wheelchair," he had complained.

"Well, Stuart, you're going to have to show them what you CAN do for them and convince them that they need your services. Why, goodness me, Stu, you can use your arms, drive your own car, and, well frankly, if I can work for a living, you sure can too."

By the time Stuart was ready to leave, Bob had hired him to serve as a deliveryman for papers being exchanged between the two offices and to run errands for them. Stuart and his wife Betty spent many hours in the evenings with Bob; oftentimes playing cards and developed.a lasting friendship between them. Stuart proved to be indispensable and a right-hand man for the business and for Bob.

The offices ran smoothly for a while but after a particularly hard end of the month close out, Bob realized he needed a part time worker, to work with the end of the month business. His ad in the Tribune brought many people looking for employment, but no one seemed the right person for Bob. He was getting quite discouraged but one day an applicant answered the ad and Bob was interested in what she had to say. He asked her to come to his office for a personal interview. When she arrived, Bob watched in surprise as she pulled crutches from the back seat of her car.

After greeting him pleasantly, she apologized for not telling him that she used crutches to walk, but admitted to needing the job really badly. She was afraid he would turn her down if she told him on the phone that she couldn't walk without crutches..

Bob let out a peal of laughter and answered, "Don't worry about that. I didn't tell you on the phone that I can't walk either, did I?" It was a cinch from then on: Miss Lillian was hired and became one of his most loved and trusted employees.

Bob found that he could reach his clients most often in the evenings so he gradually weaned himself away from going to the club. Although he was sorely missed, his friends stayed in close touch via telephone. Through the weekdays, he buried himself in his business. He had a mental list of telephone numbers of his very dearest friends that he would call every night. He usually started the conversations with a friendly "Hello," followed by, "I just wanted to touch base with you." and the conversations would follow the events of the day or wherever his mood directed them.

He continued to follow the progress of his friends and even followed up on referrals of newly–disabled people. His success with counseling became an obsession, and he seemed to thrive on helping them through their various and assorted problems.

He had long since forgotten his own inability to get around and continued to read the paper for stories of people, like himself, who for various reasons, accidents, or sicknesses, found themselves dependent on others for their day-to-day existence. He was a living example of how important it is to never give up. His constant sense of humor and soft convincing voice proved to be invaluable tools with each one.

~

One day when he was in a melancholy mood he asked if I knew how he would like to be remembered. "I'd love to be remembered as the great communicator, for everything I do is through communicating by word of mouth." He hesitated before completing his thought. "Only one problem. President Ronald Reagan earned that title first!" He went on to tell me how much he admired him and how he often thought of Mr. Reagan as his mentor. He enjoyed a good laugh before finishing his thoughts. "I sure am reaching high on the totem pole to reach for someone like the president to pattern my life after. I forget sometimes that I am just a poor old Quad pushing my luck!"

16

Bob was told one day about a young man who had opened his own agency in West Tampa and who was a quadriplegic like himself. He was having a difficult time with an unexpected spurt of growth in his insurance business at the same time that he suffered a downturn in his health, Bob took his phone number and at the first opportunity gave him a call.

Another business associate, Joe Sanchez, was also brought into our small group by Les Rosenblatt. Joe and I formed Baker-Sanchez & Associates, Inc. in 1965 and our 31 year association has been profitable and enjoyable. We have had some exciting experiences, both business and social. You can read about some of his many accomplishments in the previous article and the small one enclosed.

Les was also a quadriplegic that took me under his wing and taught me about insurance and instilled most of my strong and correct business practices. The business principles I learned from him served me very well to this day. He is mentioned prominently in the previous article I sent you.

The insurance business has been very good to me and provided me a comfortable income for most of these thirty eight years – I can hardly believe it has been that long.

There was an instant bond made between Bob and Joe. After much deliberation on both of their parts, and many long conversations, they decided to form a partnership. This proved beneficial to both and their friendship grew as the months and years passed. Bob and Joe spent many hours on the phone together, talking about their business as well as discussing their similar health problems.

Someone teased Bob one day about starting his own company for disabled people. He took the teasing good-naturedly and finally admitted to them "I have gotten so much help along the way, I think it is about time I started giving something back. You have to have traveled the road that goes on and on with no turns, to know what it is like. I have been there," he went on, "and I could never have found my way back to living again without someone to help me."

He looked around his new surroundings and was soon lost in deep thought. The idea of owning his own brick home was almost more than he could fathom. It had always been a vivid dream in his head but with so little to bank on, deep down he had wondered if it would ever come true.

He looked into my eyes as he thought of the wonder of it all, as if hoping for my understanding.

> *In the late '50s and early '60s I started buying some small real estate, in my own neighborhood at first, and then gradually ventured into other nearby areas. This has proved to be an interesting, and sometimes profitable endeavor. This happened very gradually over the years, but at one time I had as many as 8 houses, plus a 7-unit apartment house. It turned out that some of these properties "had me"*

and not nearly all of them were profitable. I have disposed of all of these houses except a few rentals that are located right in my neighborhood. They continue to be a serious problem at times, so I will be selling as soon as practical. I still have the old family home on the next street that was mostly built by my Mom. That will probably be the last, and most painful, to part with.

One of his neighbors dropped in for a short visit one day. While talking, he asked Bob if he wanted to rent his mother's old house as he had had an inquiry about it. It took Bob a few days to make the decision about the house as he had always thought it might upset his mother. The next time his neighbor came to see him, Bob agreed to rent it out, providing he was able to meet the people first. He didn't want anyone living in it who wouldn't take good care of it.

He was pleased when the renters brought him his first rental check promptly, when it was due. They also, brought news that the little house next door to his mother's had a for sale sign on it. He sent his nurse over to tell the owners to come to see him as he might be interested in buying it.

He discovered after having it inspected that he would have to make some minor repairs. He called his friend who did minor house repairs and asked for an estimate of the work needed to make the house rentable.. Bob bought the house, had it repaired and it was rented within the month. When he received two rental checks at the end of the month, he decided this dabbling in real estate was a pretty good deal.

17

Bob was not surprised to see the postman walk right by the mailbox and ring the doorbell. The postman loved to visit with Bob when they both had time. They smiled broadly at each other through the glass door and the postman entered the office. He walked to Bob's side and held up an envelope before taking the stack of mail to the secretary.

"Looks like it's a letter from your Dad," he said quietly, laying it on the extension on Bob's stretcher. It had been many years since they'd last heard from him.

Bob called for his mother and asked the nurse to return him to his bedroom. His Mother looked at the envelope, puzzled, then their eyes met and they both laughed. They had long since given up all hopes of hearing from him again. Her hands were shaking when she opened it and her voice was scarcely audible as she read the letter aloud to Bob. His Dad had been in Saudi Arabia all this time working with a large contracting firm. He had saved a nice chunk of money and was ready to come home and share it with them. He wanted them to become a family again.

Their eyes met again and lingered before she could finish reading the shocking news. Finally, with eyes twinkling with tears she said to Bob, "Aw, we don't need him."

"Just a minute, Mom, maybe he needs us."

Bob chuckled, "Boy, will he ever be surprised!" Suddenly, he was overcome with a desire to show his Dad what he and his little eighty-pound Mom had accomplished while he was away. With tears still streaming from her eyes and with feelings of anticipation, she finally agreed that they should let him come home.

For the next few days, the thick cloud of nervousness that hung over them was dotted with sudden outbursts of silly giggles when their eyes met at unexpected moments. Their tensions grew with each passing day as was evidenced by Bob's uncharacteristic snapping at his nurses and office help. His mother fell under Bob's scathing temper one day when he saw that she was dusting the same piece of furniture the second or third time.

When he called her attention to it, they laughed at how foolish they were to get so uptight over his father coming home.

"You gonna make Dad a special coming home dinner?" he finally asked.

"Oh sure," she responded quickly. "He always loved fried chicken and mashed potatoes and maybe I will bake him some biscuits, too."

"And don't forget how he liked chocolate cake for desert," Bob added.

Suddenly, they started laughing. Both were hoping everything would turn out all right.

An unusual calmness settled over the house the day his dad arrived. His mother had set the table in the dining room for the first time since they had moved into their new home. Bob remembered how upset his dad used to get when he had to watch his son be fed, so Bob insisted that his nurse feed him in his room while his mother and dad had a quiet dinner for two in the dining room. His mother finally acquiesced and all plans were set.

Bob would never forget the look of bewilderment on his dad's face when he entered his room that day. Neither would he ever forget the tension that filled the room when he saw his dad walk into the room. But even more engraved in his memory was the picture of his mother and dad coming from the dining room, to Bob's room a short while later with their plates piled high with his mother's southern cooked delicacies. His father would have no part of the fancy dining room. He wanted to eat dinner with his son.

They lingered over the dinner as long as possible and then they began to share each other's adventures of the past years. They played catch-up until they had covered most of the bases.

"Would you like to take a tour through the house," his mother asked, smiling with anticipation. They left Bob and walked together from one room to another. She pointed out each of the features that she liked most. His father was astounded at what they had accomplished. When they were finished with the inspection, they returned to Bob's room. Both were smiling broadly.

"Do you really need an office that big?" his dad teased. "Sure is nice! And I see you even have a computer." Bob was beaming with pride.

"This is a lot of house, Bob, but I like your room the best of all. Great idea to put in the big window. I can't believe what you have done here."

Suddenly, he reached in his pocket and pulled out a tired looking check. "I've been saving as much as I could every since I have been gone." he said proudly. "And the best news of all is that I was transferred to a job here in the States. It will be too far for me to commute daily, but I can find a place to stay near the job weekdays, and then come home every Friday night to spend the weekend with you all."

He walked over and put his arm around Bob's shoulders. "I am really proud of you, Son. You have come a long way boy, since the last time I saw you."

When Bob shared with me the details of their first night as a family, his eyes watered up. "We will never know who gave whom the biggest shock: Dad with his big check and changed attitude, or me and mom in our new home and with all our changes. That was the first time I ever heard my dad say he was proud of me and I shall never, ever forget it."

Bob's father was an avid fisherman. He asked one day if I liked to eat fish. He said he had exhausted his neighbors appetite by bringing them so many undressed fish after his frequent trips down to Lake Okeechobee. His laugh sounded like Bob's when he went on to tell me how they still enjoyed fresh fish, but only if he took time to clean them.

"Hey, I interrupted," you can call me anytime day or night and I will come right over and pick them up. We love fresh fish. And, don't worry about dressing them. My husband and I will be glad to take care of that little matter." I assured him.

The phone call interrupted our sleep at two o'clock one morning. It was Bob, laughing and apologizing for calling at this hour, but his dad had just come in from a fishing trip and had a mess of fish for me. I thanked him and told him we would be right over to get them. We dragged ourselves out of bed and drove to Bob's house.

His mother met us at the door grinning. We walked back to Bob's room and found him propped up on his elbows, with his dad's fishing hat sitting jauntily on the back of his head. His dad's fishing rod was propped on the side of his bed. "We had a good trip," Bob quickly said. "We've got you a mess of fish."

I looked in shock at the galvanized tub on the floor, just teeming with little blue gill bream. I quickly produced the pan I had brought to retrieve my mess of fish. Bob laughed when he saw it and said, "Oh no, these are ALL for you."

My husband stood near by with a long face and shaking his head. With Mr. Baker's help they carried the tub of fish to our car and put them in the trunk. As we were driving home we could almost hear Bob laughing.

We saw the sun coming up over the horizon just as we were finishing the last of the little pan fish, the largest of which was the size of my hand. My husband grudgingly helped me make room in the freezer for our mess of fish. He looked at the sky and asked if he could go back to bed now. "I would have thrown these little bastards in the garbage if anyone but Bob Baker had given this many to us." I heard the water running in the shower shortly after as my husband prepared to clean up and take a short nap before going to work. Bob laughed all over again each time he recalled the fun it had been to pull such a joke on us.

I would always smile and say, "That was some MESS OF FISH all right!"

The Dear Frances Letter

Bob's life with his mom and dad soon settled back into some form of normalcy, with each weekend bringing forth a warm exchange of ideas between them as they shared the past week's happenings. At his dad's request, dinners were always served in Bob's room. His mother had purchased TV tables for them and Bob's nurse continued to assist him with his food as needed. Sharing ideas and plans for their futures followed after each evening meal.

Through their weekend exchanges, Bob discovered again that his dad was a wonderful man and that they had a lot to talk about. One evening they got into a hot discussion about the little frame houses in their neighborhood. They were trying to figure some way to buy them and after minor renovations and a little paint, they both agreed it might be a good investment to use them for rental properties.

This happiness was not to last. Their plans soon came to a shocking halt. His father was killed in an automobile accident as he was returning home one Friday night. He had made a right hand turn on a curve of a very slippery road and lost control of his car. This was the most devastating and unsettling thing Bob had experienced since his own accident. He couldn't believe that his Dad would not be coming home to them. He and his Mom were alone again and the weekends that followed were so painful they could hardly endure them.

When I would visit him and ask how he was feeling, he would answer, "I am as low as a snake's belly today." I was to get used to that remark and know exactly what it meant, as he struggled to accept his loss.

It wasn't long after Bob's father died that Ray, my husband of thirty-nine years, died suddenly of a massive heart attack. Several weeks later I received a letter in the mail. The writing on the envelope gave me no clue as to whom it was from. When I opened it, I was startled to see words scribbled all over the yellow legal paper. The signature at the bottom caught my eye before I had read the message. It was signed in big bold print, "Love Bob."

He had written a few labored lines telling me that in lieu of flowers for Ray, he was sending me his undying love. And, should I ever need anything, to remember he would always be there for me. I thought I had already hit the bottom of the barrel of my tears, but this unleashed a fresh bucket full. He was, without a doubt, one of the dearest friends a person could have.

He told me later how many weeks and how many trash cans full of discarded letters it took for him to write this brief message in his own handwriting. He admitted it was his first attempt at letter writing since his accident 31 years ago. I took turns wiping his wet eyes and then mine as we cried together over my loss.

After my husband's death, he started calling me every night. When we were at a loss for words, he would ask if I had worked that day's crossword puzzle. He always enjoyed working them with his nurse, but when they came across a word they didn't know he would have her give me a call. I can remember one night when we were working the puzzle together and we came across a clue that that defied my imagination. I could not figure out what the word could be It was a five-letter word, possibly beginning with "s," and the clue was "hair piece for ladies." He started laughing, and I thought he would never stop. "It is sometimes worn by men too," he said between chuckles.

"Well, I just don't know," I finally admitted.

"The word is snood, Dottie."

"Aw, Come on, Bob, is there such a word?" I retorted. "I never heard of it before."

"Why of course. I wear a snood on my head every night when the weather is cold. Guess you never knew that since my accident, my body has no thermostat and the snood on my head helps to control my body temperature in cold weather." We were laughing heartily at the end of the discussion.

18

The sound of pots and pans rattling in the kitchen awakened Bob.

"Hey, Mom! Aren't you going to come say good morning to me?"

"I'm going to the store," she told him, while walking toward the door.

"No, Mother," Bob told her quickly. "We don't need anything from the store this morning. And I need my coffee."

"We do too," she answered, turning quickly back to the kitchen.

She was back in no time, holding a glass of water in her hand. "Why don't you get out of that bed, you lazy bum?" Her eyes were shooting daggers at him as she stood over him. "All you ever do is lay on that bed and ask me to wait on you. You just get up and get your own coffee!"

Bob was at a loss as to how to answer her, but finally said, "Wish I could, Mom." Then, realizing that laughter always worked with her, he attempted a big open-mouthed laugh, but all he could muster was a smile and a soft chuckle. "Put the water on the table," he told her, "I will need it when I take my pills."

Her eyes met his and suddenly she laughed. "Oh, all right," and she turned and reentered the kitchen, carrying the glass of water with her, muttering something that Bob couldn't understand.

Bob lay on the bed staring at the ceiling for a while, wondering what in the world he could do for his Mother. He knew she was getting much worse as her "trips" into "Never Never" Land and away from lucidity were coming more often. His problem was that she always looked the same and he was never quite sure if she were teasing him or if she had gone off again.

He was still deep in thought. when he heard his mother coming back into the room. He wished he could turn his head and look at her but he had to wait until she walked into his line of vision.

Suddenly, she appeared, carrying a tray with his breakfast on it. He saw at a glance that she had made him a bowl of cereal and milk, two pieces of buttered toast on a saucer with a big dollop of grape jelly on the side and an unpeeled banana. The coffee was steaming in the cup on the tray. She placed the tray on the bedside table and left the room without offering to assist him with his breakfast.

Bob told me later that he just lay there and looked at the cup of coffee and food as he thought to himself, "This has to be the perfect definition of the true meaning of loneliness." He waited for the morning nurse to come on duty.

"Good morning Bob," she greeted him happily when she arrived. Immediately she noticed the uneaten food on the table. "What's the matter with my favorite patient this morning? Not hungry?"

"No, not much." He answered. Then he told her about his mother being all confused again and what had happened.

～

It was early morning and Bob was waiting for his Mom to bring his coffee, which had become their normal routine.

"Hey Mom," he called out to her. "Where's my coffee?"

She scolded him with her eyes and a shrug of the shoulders and returned to the kitchen. Only a couple of minutes lapsed when she reentered his room carrying a tray with a glass of water on it. Her little black bag was hanging over one shoulder. Without a word , his mother walked out the front door.

Bob pounded the bell, pinned on the sheet under his hand until the nurse came running in.

"What's up, Bob?" he asked, while walking to the foot of the bed to get in Bob's line of vision.

"Mom's acting strangely. Think she may be trying to go to the store again. She just walked out the door. Would you check on her, please?"

His mother ignored him when she came back through the door to Bob's room with the nurse holding her hand. She walked straight back to her bedroom, removed her damp tennis shoes, climbed into bed and fell asleep. Bob stayed in bed, staring at the ceiling for about two hours.

The nurse sat on the small chair by his bed, discussing his mother's condition. He told Bob he had found his mother sitting in the flowerbed behind the house, clutching her purse with one hand and pulling up little weeds with the other. He told him she gave him no resistance and came willingly back into the house with him.

"But, even worse, I found her tennis shoes in the oven."

"You haven't had your breakfast yet," the nurse said while walking toward the kitchen. He returned shortly to show Bob that his mother had made his breakfast after all, but had forgotten to bring it to him.

"That's what is so puzzling about her behavior. One minute she is with us and before you can say Scat, she is gone again to wherever she goes to escape from whatever she is running from. I can't figure it out." Bob commented sadly. "I have picked up one clue on her behavior though Her black bag seems to be her security blanket. When she puts it over her shoulder, I just know she is off in outer space again."

"I am really worried about her, Bob. She needs an attendant more than you do."

"I know what you mean and I can't always see what she is doing or where she is going. I'm calling the doctor as soon as his office opens," Bob concluded with a frown.

Bob called the doctor that same day and the doctor was adamant that he needed to do something about his mother. As Bob was considering his options, his thoughts were interrupted by a phone call from his office. He answered their business questions and in the next breath he was telling the nurse how good all of his staff were about helping with his mother.

"I know," the nurse agreed. But they don't have eyes in the back of their heads and sometimes they get busy and forget. I think your mother needs to be in a protected environment."

"You mean I need to put her in a nursing home, don't you?" Bob snapped. "Mom and I promised each other years ago that we would always be here for each other and that we would never put the other in a home."

"But it is the kindest thing you could do for her, Bob. She is no longer capable of making decisions for herself and as much as you want to keep her in her home, your circumstances are such that it has become impossible. It isn't safe for her to be free to go at her own will wherever she wants to go."

Bob called the doctor shortly after their conversation, only to be told the same thing the nurse had told him. He finally agreed with the doctor and told him he would get his friends to research the local nursing facilities, as he wanted the very best for his Mom. He told the nurse that he didn't want any breakfast. "Please just get me some coffee." He spent the rest of the morning calling friends to ask about referrals to nursing homes. He told me later that he had been procrastinating and just spinning his wheels because deep down inside he simply wanted to keep his mother at home.

He finally reached one of his neighbors who he had spent a lot of time with as a child. Bob hadn't known that his wife had died several years before, after a long confinement in a nursing facility. His friend told him of the beautiful grounds surrounding the facility that she lived in for three years, the giant oaks and well-groomed hedges and spacious lawns. He said that many times the nurses would take the patients for walks and let them visit the gardens and watch the butterflies and birds. His old neighbor had been well pleased with the loving care they had given his wife and he would heartily recommend this particular Center to anyone.

Bob felt somewhat relieved just knowing that there was such a place just a few miles from his home and went to sleep that night with a measure of satisfaction that his decision was almost made.

The next day was one of her better days. When she came to sit by his bed and chat, she was well dressed; hair neatly combed. He observed her very carefully and all seemed normal. She made and served his breakfast, making small talk as she went back and forth to the kitchen.. Bob called in to his office and told the secretary he was running a little late, but to call him any time they needed him. The nurse teased him about being too tired to come to work. She kidded him about staying out too late the night before and asked who was his hot date?

Her calm behavior that particular day was almost as confusing to Bob as the opposite had been the day before.

Bob turned to his mother and asked her to stay with him for a while so they could just talk. They had a most enjoyable few hours and then Bob rang for his nurse to get him dressed.

Preparing for the office in the morning simply meant getting a sponge bath, changing the urine bag and putting clean sheets on the stretcher, then, a shift from his bed to the stretcher. All heavy procedures and baths were done in the evenings. Bob had discovered that wearing pajamas often created skin problems so most of the time he lay nude with only a sheet or blanket wrapped around him. Before clients came in, the nurse would often wrap a nice soft towel over his shoulders to at least give him the semblance of being dressed.

Bob was wearing the familiar smile on his face when they took him into his office. No one would know by casually looking at him, the hell he was going through.

He was having an especially difficult Saturday a few weeks later, when he discovered Charles Karault with his wonderful travel program on TV. Charles Karault provided a much-needed diversion from the stresses of worrying about his mother. From that day on, Bob traveled with Charles to see the countryside every Saturday.

When his many friends went on trips or vacations after that, he insisted on having their itinerary with times of arrivals and departures. He wanted a full accounting of all travel plans. In his mind, he traveled with them every mile of the way. At times he was able to visualize what they were seeing as he had sometimes traveled that same country with his good friend Charles Karault. We often teased Bob about traveling so much.

19

The day finally came for my much-needed vacation. My three sisters and I had a week at the beach planned. Bob was happy to know that we were going to be together for a few days, but as always, he insisted on knowing the name of the beach and the hotel in which we would be staying, as well as a phone number where he could reach us if need be.

After a day of walking the beach and collecting seashells, we returned to our rooms for a nice dinner and to relax by reminiscing about our childhood. I was approaching sixty years of age with my sisters ranging up to eighty. As we took turns recalling funny incidents, the sharp and urgent ring of the telephone interrupted our laughter. We looked at each other anxiously as we wondered which of us was about to receive bad news.

The strange male voice on the phone jerked me into listening intently, as it apologized for interrupting our nice outing at the beach, but that he would have to ask us to tone down our party a little as he had been getting complaints from the neighboring guests. I argued with him at first, trying to explain that it could not be coming from our room, as we were just four old ladies relaxing together and talking about our childhood.

"I'm sorry," the voice said, "but I have had more than one complaint."

I heard a sudden burst of laughter from the phone and in a state of shock;,I recognized Bob's voice and that of his nurse. "Just checking up on you, Dottie," he finally said. "I am already missing you." He told how his nurse had muffled his voice by putting a towel over his mouth.

～

It was a warm, humid morning and Bob realized his mother was very late bringing his breakfast.

"Hey Mom," he called to her. He heard her coming but without a word of greeting, she walked right by him and on out the front door.

Bob started franticly paging his nurse. "Hurry, Jim, Mom's gone off again." Jim rushed to the door and after looking down the street to no avail. He came back and called the police for help.

The policeman was kind and understanding. This was not the first time he had been called to find Bob's mother. He rushed back out the door and took off in his police car. The nurse tried to console Bob but his tears started to flow.

The friendly policeman found her two blocks away sitting in the middle of the street. He noted her red face and tear-filled eyes while he coaxed her gently into his car. She was able to tell him the correct house number and the street on which she lived, but said she couldn't find it. She said she was lost.

She walked lamely to Bob's side when they entered his room. He was relieved to see his dear, but confused

The Dear Frances Letter

mom home again. His mom tried to tell him between sobs that she couldn't find her way back home. Then, he noticed she was fully clothed in her little shorts and red shirt, but wearing her bra on top of the shirt. He knew then just what he had to do. He realized it was no longer safe to try to take care of her at home. He recalled how he had to sell her car because she would go to the store and get lost coming back home.

Bob dialed the doctor's number and with the assistance of the policeman called for an ambulance. They carried her to St Joseph's Hospital leaving Bob with his nurse. His mother didn't even cast a glance in his direction as they left his room.

After a week of testing, her doctor called Bob to tell him that she had an injured hip from a fall in the street, nothing serious, but that she would need special care for a little while. They had made arrangements to have her admitted to the nursing home across the street from the hospital. The doctor had determined that she was suffering with a dementia; he strongly suspected Alzheimer's disease.

Bob was beside himself for days. He couldn't sleep. He lost his appetite . It was obvious to all that he was losing weight. At the same time, he was losing interest in his business. Fortunately, he had trained his help well and they carried on by asking him questions over the intercom. Bob didn't want to get out of bed. He just wanted to lay in bed and stare at the ceiling.

Our visits became a time of crying together as he once again stewed over the decision he had made to admit his mother to the nursing home. I had trouble convincing him that it was the kindest thing he could do for her though in the end, he knew it was the only right solution. Bob's mother was transferred to this new home in just a matter of weeks.

He hadn't seen her since she had been admitted to the hospital. His friends at the funeral home heard about this and called to offer to take him out for a visit so he could take a look for himself and maybe feel better satisfied about his mother.

She didn't recognize him when they pushed his wheelchair into her room .. All attempts at making conversation with her failed but Bob sat quietly by in his wheelchair just looking at her while she stared off into space. "Mom," he finally said, "Please get better so I can take you home again."

It was like talking to the wall. She didn't even look at him. He knew there was little more that he could do for her. Tears streamed freely down his face and finally fell into his lap. He swore to himself that he would never go back to see her again unless there was a decided improvement. Bob and the driver rode in silence all the way home.

He would call often to talk with his Mother's nurse to see if she needed anything and to stay abreast of her condition. He sent her the cross-stitch picture she had worked on for one year, while sitting by his bed in the evenings, to be hung in her room in the home. He was hopeful it would lend comfort to her if and when she became aware of it.

The days and weeks dragged by. Each time he called the nursing home, he received much the same message. His mother's condition was getting worse by the day.

His mother died about eight months after that. He accepted her death with dignity, saying that he felt OK about it as she was in a much better place. He admitted that in his heart he had said goodbye to her that day when he went to see her in the nursing home. That was when he had faced the fact that she would never be able to come home again. He could see that she didn't know who she was or where she was, and her words had turned to gibberish. He told the nursing home staff to just call the Ed Jennings Funeral Home as he had already made the arrangements with them and he knew them well after the many times they had provided transportation for him.

As the time neared for her funeral, Bob kept his eyes focused on the clock. The hands on the clock seemed to go slower and slower, giving him time to dread it more and more. Finally, he had to make his decision and he knew that in his grief-stricken state, he was not fit to go to her funeral. Instead, he chose to remain at home.

His one wish was that my son Gary videotape her funeral so he could at least watch it later. Gary was visibly shaken by the solemn responsibility of taping the funeral of his friend's mother. He wanted to show close ups of the beautiful array of flowers and the faces of Bob's many friends and clients that had gathered in the chapel to bid his mother a fond farewell. His favorite nurse stayed at home with him during the funeral.

Bob chose to be alone when he first looked at the tape. He treasured it and watched it over and over. His many friends from all over the city and county dropped by his home often to help him through this most devastating time. To be totally alone with only the nurses who came and went on their different shifts was very difficult for Bob to accept. He was certain the days and nights had more hours in them and the weeks seemed like eternities. His many friends showered him with phone calls, visits and attentions of all kinds in their effort to ease his tremendous loss

20

I stopped in one Saturday with both my boys, thinking they would give Bob something different to think about. He responded to their broad smiles with one of his own. In no time he was telling them stories from his early childhood. The story that we will always remember is the one about the time when he felt rich after opening his insurance business. He had sold the biggest policy of his career to a company which was building a big high rise apartment complex on Bayshore Boulevard.

When the initial payment came in the mail, he decided it was time to do something real nice for his Mom as an expression of his love and also his appreciation for all of her help. He told them about how he had bought her a new Cadillac convertible. The day the salesperson delivered it, his mother was furious at Bob, saying they could not afford it. They finally convinced her to go try it out.

She had driven off like a demon was after her but returned in a very short time. The top was down and the seats were filled with big black trash bags. She was smiling from ear to ear when she told Bob that the old man down the street had raked the leaves from under his big oak trees and had them bagged up for the trash collector. He had helped her load them into the convertible and she was so happy to have enough to mulch all of her azalea beds across the front of their house. She would never admit to liking the new convertible.

By the time he finished the story, he was laughing heartily but with tears streaming down his cheeks. My sons were trying to hide their tears and we felt this was stressing Bob too much. We knew it was time for us to leave.

My older son, Glenn, during one of his occasional visits with Bob, brought up the subject of guns. My son was reminiscing about how long it took to save enough money to buy his first shotgun. He said that this favorite treasure still resides within his modest collection. He went on to mentioned a particular collector rifle he had been seeking.

He was taken aback when Bob said, "I have one of those. If you want it, I will make you a good price."

"How do you come by having this rifle?" Glenn asked.

"Well, I have that one and several more. You see, I also have a collection. If you want any particular specimen, I can help you find it and I can help you get it. I am a licensed firearm dealer."

Bob directed him to a shelf where the latest gun dealer trade publications were lying. "Take those with you. The new ones will arrive any day now."

My son, Glenn, called me later to recount this surprising occurrence. He said, "I wouldn't have guessed that a quadriplegic who will never be able to fire one would be a knowledgeable, up to date gun-collector!"

"But," Glenn went on, "I'll admit I have a couple that I've never fired. In fact, I imagine there are many collectors with specimens they don't fire. Now that I think about it, one of the enjoyable aspects of collecting is acquiring knowledge of the subject. Bob is very knowledgable of the technical aspects of firearms,, their history, and their marketplace. What an active mind resides in that passive body!"

My son continued his occasional visits, but with the added dimension of discussing accuracy, muzzle velocity, barrel lengths, rifling twist, powder loads, types of finishes and the many other aspects of gun collecting to make it even more enjoyable for both of them. He was forever amazed at the vast knowledge Bob had stored up about guns, along with his other interests.

21

His mother's passing made Bob think of his own mortality. After a few weeks had passed he made a strange request of me. He wanted my help in planning his own funeral. He wanted it to be simple, he had said. And he needed to make the arrangements while he could.

He was in a very serious mood that day and neither of us knew exactly where to start. Finally, we agreed that to start with the selection of the funeral home would be the most likely place. With that, he dialed the owner of the funeral home; the same one who had provided him with so much transportation through the years and also who had been in charge of his mother's funeral. He joined us at Bob's home in a very short time, bringing catalogues with prices and colored pictures of caskets. Questions were asked and Bob supplied the answers. He, of course, would be laid to rest in the same plot with his mother and father.

Bob heaved a big sigh of relief when Ed left and we were alone again. Ed had told Bob to be thinking of what hymns he would like used at his funeral. He would pick them up later.

"I don't want the music to be only hymns" Bob said emphatically." There are other songs that I really love."

"Name a few and I'll write the titles down." I suggested.

The Dear Frances Letter

"How about *Bridge Over Troubled Waters*? I love that song. And another one that I love is *Help Me Through The Night*, He thought a few minutes before listing *The Impossible Dream, Sweet Memories,* and *He.* He concluded with *How Great Thou Art, May The Good Lord Bless and Keep you* and *Amazing Grace.* "There may be a few more when I have more time to think about it."

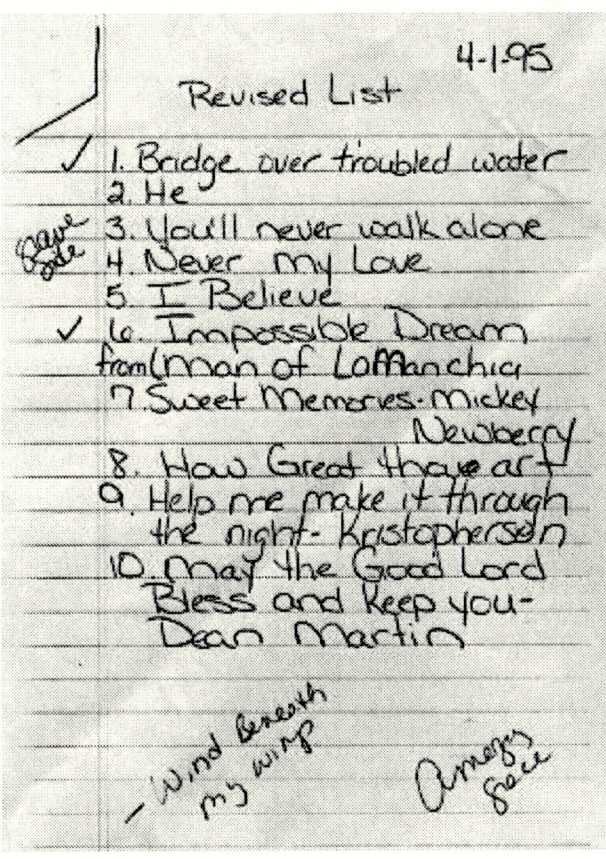

I looked at him and said: "But that may be too many, Bob."

"Oh yeah," he snapped. "Who says?"

I smiled and fastened my eyes onto his. "Well, how many songs do you think they sing at a person's funeral?"

"I don't know. I have never been to a funeral."

He quickly amended that by saying, "Of course I attended Mom's funeral, by way of video tape."

"Well," I suggested gently "let's make that list a little shorter. OK?"

"Wait a minute, Young Lady. Whose funeral are we planning, yours or mine?" I wiped away my tears and before we knew it, we broke out in nervous laughter as we realized how foolish we were to fuss over such a delicate matter. We both knew we had to either laugh or cry, so laugh we did.

"I tell you what, Bob, you can have as many songs as you would like." I conceded. I patted him on the forehead and said goodbye, leaving the room before I choked to death on my tears.

He called the next day to thank me for helping him with the funeral arrangements. "And you are not going to like this but I added one more song to our list."

"My mother loved *You Are The Wind Beneath My Wings*. I want that to be the last song and I want it dedicated to my mother. She was truly the wind beneath my wings, you know."

"That's wonderful ,Bob, and I will see that it is done."

"But you won't have to worry with that," he quickly said. "I am having my secretary put it in writing and will give it to Ed to pack away with the other plans until it is needed."

"I called Ed this morning and made another request."

"You did?" I asked.

"Yeah. I asked him to get the largest limo that he could find to transport my extended family to the funeral." I could visualize a smile on his face and almost see his blue eyes twinkling as he went on. "I asked him to see that a bottle of champagne all iced down was placed in the limo so that you all can drink a toast to the wonderful life I have had. I don't want any tears when I go to meet my Maker and Mom and Dad and Bunny. I want you all to celebrate the wonderful life I have lived and not my death. I'll bet few people have had it so good!"

I gulped back my tears and said, "Bob, you're crazy!"

He laughed and said, "You sound just like my mom. She used to tell me when we were pondering how and why I was living so much longer than anybody expected, "You're so mean the Good Lord don't want you and the devil won't have you." Don't know where she picked that one up, but she used it quite often when she was cross with me."

We were silent for a while, listening to each other's unspoken words. I smiled through my tears as best I could.

"This isn't easy, you know." I finally said. I saw him give a couple of big gulps before concluding, "I know, I know. I hope I haven't upset you."

His kind words spoken in such a soft and understanding voice broke the dam that had been holding back my tears. I could tell that he was crying too.

Bob finally broke the long silence by asking for another favor. "I feel so relieved to have all that taken care of and behind me. Thanks to my wonderful attorney and friend, I have my house all in order now, too. But, there's one more thing that bugs me."

"Name it," I quickly replied.

"Well, you know that many people have been really good to me. People have become my passion, and I wish I could think of some way to convey to a lot of them just how much their friendship has meant to me. Many have done things for me that they considered small at the time, but to me, they were huge and sometimes it was like a prayer answered. I am thinking now of two of my paramedic friends who used to come in the evenings and play cards with me. I recall one night when we were just hanging out and the subject came up as to where I was born. Newport, Tennessee, I told them, though I had never been back there since I was a little boy, even though my grandfather still lived there up in the mountains. Somehow, we all decided we should make that trip back to my childhood home before my aged grandfather passed away."

"Much to my mothers chagrin, plans were made and Grandpa paid the expenses while I left the driving to my friends. I went to my first beer party on top of Grandpa's mountain with those two fellows and what a party it was! They drank the beer and told dirty jokes while I supplied the laughter to egg them on. I sure would love to write them a note to thank them and tell them what pleasure that effort of theirs has given me through the years - enough to last a lifetime."

22

"Well Bob, why don't you dictate the letters to your secretary and get her to mail it to them?"

"I have thought about that," he quickly added, "but to tell you the truth, there are some things that are too personal and private to let my staff know. I need to find somebody who I can trust and someone who doesn't know the people I am writing to."

I pondered over that for some time before I thought of the ideal person. I called Bob the next day to recommend my cousin. She had spent most of her life doing accounting work and could be trusted implicitly to follow his orders and keep everything he dictated to her a secret. Also, she was very good at shorthand and typing. They started the following week with Carolyn working as many hours as her permanent job would allow. Bob's reports on her work were glowing and he loved her on first sight. He said he felt comfortable with her and found he could express his thoughts to her without having to worry about anything. She was so cute. He loved her beautiful red hair and natural good looks but most of all he enjoyed her giggles, which she did at every available opportunity. "I think I am in love again," he admitted after a few weeks of working with her.

She would take the dictation and return to her home to write the letters on fine linen stationary. The next time she came she placed the letter on the little wooden tray that had been custom made to allow his best viewing. After he had read and approved them, he had her seal them in his presence and put a postage stamp on each one to be mailed at a later date. They had such fun working together and often ended their sessions by having "take-out" lunches and a nice relaxed visit afterwards.

When all of his thank-you and bequest letters were written, Bob had her tie them up with blue ribbon. Atop the stack of letters was a simple request that they be dropped in the mail promptly after his death. When they had finished the last letter, he asked her to take them to his attorney's office to be stored for safekeeping.

~Tribune photograph by Candace C. Mundy~

One day while visiting Bob, I noticed he was in a rather pensive mood. He was staring out into nowhere in particular.

"You know something," he said slowly, dropping his eyes to the floor. "There are just some things that I can't change." He was staring at a spot in front of the office door. "Look at that," he quickly added. "See that little piece of fluff. It has been there for two days. Every time someone comes in the door, or leaves, it moves back and forth with the airflow."

I rose quickly to go pick it up, but he stopped me. "No, don't move it! I want to see how long it will take for the girls to see it and to remove it. My mom would never allow a spot on the floor when she was with me."

I patted him on the forehead, knowing he was missing his mother again.

23

When Bob found time on his hands, he started to worry about what would happen to him when he got old. He knew of the many health complications that could occur with age and his condition. He tried to estimate his cost of maintaining a life at home or even if he should he be institutionalized. He couldn't get away from the shocking results. As he fretted over them, he knew he had best do something.

He placed a call to one of the companies who had provided his health .insurance. He asked if the company had any provisions among their many policies that would cover such expenses. He was passed from one level of the company to another until finally, he found himself talking with one of the Vice Presidents at the top.

The VP was very interested and asked Bob to put his ideas in writing and send them to him for further consideration. Bob spent many hours with his secretary, putting his ideas into a formal proposal to the insurance company.. As soon as it was completed, Bob felt better just knowing they would consider it.

Weeks passed before he heard from the company. The news was very encouraging. But, they first needed proof of demand for this special needs health insurance coverage. If it proved to be practical, then Bob would be able to sell such policies. He was told that it would be very expensive, but Bob knew that those same costs

The Dear Frances Letter

coming out of his pocket and others like him would be almost prohibitive. He lost no time in contacting his many friends throughout the county and state who might someday need this type of insurance.

The enthusiasm from those who had back injuries and were in need of constant medical attention and ever-changing appliancies was overwhelming. It seems most of them had been living under the same cloud of fear that Bob had.

When he relayed this news to the home office, they gave him the green light and Bob began laying the groundwork for his new project. He was the first person to purchase this form of coverage from that company. This proved to be a good purchase endorsement and helped Bob to sell the policies. The home office personnel were amazed at his success and were very complimentary. He began to take a renewed interest in his business.

He told me later, when all was settled with the new insurance, "You know, I'm a little embarrassed to tell you this, but I honestly think I have a pipeline to the Good Lord. When I lay my problems on Him, I don't hear His voice but I know in my heart I will be able to arrive at a decision, or find a solution before too long. I get amused, at times when the Old Man up there doesn't grant my wish. I find myself wondering why, and most often, if I wait long enough, I can see that it would not have been the best answer for me anyway."

24

It was only a few weeks later that Bob read an article about voice-controlled computer software called "Dragon Dictate"™ and became fascinated by it. After toying with the idea he purchased one and set forth to learn to use the voice activated word-processor. This proved to be a very big challenge for him. After many hours of frustration and weeks of determined labor, he began to feel that it was worthwhile.

I recall one day when I paid him an unexpected visit. I found him in front of the computer, red faced and his eyes blurred with anger. When I asked what was wrong, He yelled out at me," If this damn machine screws me up one more time, I'm getting off this stretcher and kicking the devilish thing clear out of my house!"

"Join the club, Bob, you are becoming a real, true computer user."

Before the year had passed, he was able to send e-mails to his friends and on special occasions, he would answer business letters. He had gotten quite adept at using the word processor. In fact, his letter to his nurse, Frances, was written using this computer system. It had taken him three weeks to complete it, he admitted to her in the letter, but he was hopeful of finally making contact with her.

His secretary, responding to his enthusiasm, went through his photograph album and together they selected pictures (all of which appear in this book) that most closely depicted his physical and medical condition at the time of the writings. He was so very proud and printed off a copy of the letter, the same one I had placed in the box, tied with blue ribbons and hidden away on the top shelf of my closet for safe keeping.

His charge nurse, Nancy, had impeccable skills taking care of quadriplegics but he soon learned that nursing was where her skills stopped. She prepared a few of his evening meals and it wasn't long before he knew they had to figure out another means of getting his dinners.

She was delighted to be relieved of this responsibility and lost no time in locating a nearby family restaurant, which she passed each evening as she was coming to work the night shift. They both liked this new arrangement as she could call from the restaurant and read Bob the menu, allowing him to make his own choices of the evening meal.

It became a standing joke between them: Whenever he would place his phone order for dinner, he would always end it with "…double the mashed potatoes and hold the peas." He almost lost his appetite each time he would see English peas on the plate. He thought there should be a law against serving peas to anyone in bed.

All too many times, when a pea had rolled off the spoon and gotten lost in his covers, he could visualize a large green bug with legs and feelers crawling across his body without him being able to feel it or see it. When they had rumpled up his bed, in their mad search for the little pea, Bob could imagine lying on a white sheet with a large green spot on it for all to see when they came to visit him. He often wondered if there was one more pea hidden under his covers.

After that, whenever ordering his dinner over the phone, he'd end with "Double the potatoes and hold the peas, please."

25

It was in the early 1990's that Bob's health began to fail. Sherrie Dulworth, now working in New York, flew in to oversee his care and to be with him in the hospital. He had several long visits in intensive care for treatments and he was forced to make the decision to go along with his doctor's recommendations. What he had long feared would finally come to pass: He would live on a respirator for the rest of his life.

When Bob came home from the hospital, his doctor had done the tracheotomy and he was connected to a respirator with a prognosis of "...maybe six weeks or so". (They had made an incision in his throat to remove secretions and allow for the tracheotomy.) Little did he know at that time that over the next few years he would be returning to the hospital for various reasons, usually pneumonia or severe kidney or bladder infections.

Going to the hospital always upset his normal routine and was disorienting for Bob. He always fought being admitted as long as he could and tried to be medically managed at home with home health nurses. But even with this assistance, Bob continued to call the shots in his own life, often to the dismay (and over strenuous objections) of his doctors who were, no doubt, accustomed to more docile patients.

We never knew how long we should stay when we visited Bob, in spite of his begging us not to leave. We would watch as he chewed his words and spit them out before gasping for another breath. We could tell he was trying to synchronize his words with the machine purring at his side. Lest we not understand, he would purse his mouth in such a way that we could at least read his lips. We often saw frustration when a sentence was left hanging in the air, incomplete, or even worse when he had to swallow in the middle of a word and need to repeat it. He would roll his eyes upward and struggle to give us a smile. Since he could no longer leave his house or go out into the world, he had welcomed company who would bring the world into him. He said he just soaked up every word that was spoken and always hated to see time pass.

"Time passes fast, you know, when you're having fun."

It was nearly a week before Bob could talk again as he struggled to get used to breathing with the help of the machine. He had to learn to inhale and exhale and speak in coordination with the machine. His timing was often off and the words just would not come out clearly. This was quite a challenge for him and required many hours of practicing. This was really tough for a man who, in his own mind, wanted to be remembered as a great communicator like the man he admired so much, his President, Mr. Ronnie Reagan. We made him a board on which was printed the words he would most often need. His secretary compiled a list of phone numbers of favorite friends and other frequently called numbers. With these two aids he was able to make his wishes known by pointing without wasting his breath by trying to speak.

When his friends called the hospital, they talked first with the nurse who gave the latest report on his condition, then she would hold the phone to his ear for him to hear what we had to say.

At long last, he was finally able to go home but he found things very different. It was far more difficult to manage his business since he required much more rest and personal care and constant use of the respirator. Due to a variety of health complications, Bob's doctor forbade him going the few feet away to work in his office. Bob obeyed the doctor's orders but was very unhappy about having to stay in bed. He found the routines with the machine more and more aggravating.

Although the girls in the office kept him abreast of the happenings each day, he was itching to get back on the job. He increased his time with the breathing exercises and gradually, he could begin to feel a difference. He pushed himself until the nurse worried that he was overtaxing himself. She finally called the doctor and enlisted his aid in slowing Bob down with his therapy. Bob was delighted to find that the doctor thought what he was doing was wonderful and had told the nurse that his determination and persistence was producing good results.

Bob was getting more in tune with the respirator by this time. When we commended him on the wonderful progress he was making, he always came back at us with his own special quip. One day, he surprised me by saying, "If someone could invent a respirator that would breath for me as fast as I want to talk, they would really have something to brag about. I get so mad sometimes when I have to swallow or gasp for air, leaving what I was saying hanging in the air, or even worse when it happens in the middle of a word." I assured him that it worried him a lot more than it bothered us who were listening.

In record-breaking time, he was returning to his office for two hours at a time. As he played catch-up with the many details he had missed, two hours didn't seem long enough. He frequently fudged a little and worked overtime on the job. He no longer took care of scheduling his nurses, but had hired a charge nurse to take over those details.

It was almost catastrophic when for various reasons new nurses had to be hired. Their interviews involved Bob to the extent that he often felt like a guinea pig as the charge nurse taught them the various things that he needed, using him as a live example. In most cases they had to be taught to take care of the tube in his throat and the respirator. Along with this specialized training, they needed to know what was expected of them with his meals. Bob really hated changes but he could quickly decide by the end of the new nurse's training period whether he would be satisfied or not. These training periods sometimes lasted three day or more, but it was not unusual for Bob to say, "this is not going to work," and they would have to call in another applicant.

In the meantime, he was able to buy a couple more houses in his neighborhood and to keep his handyman working, unstopping toilets, patching leaks and the multitude of other minor repairs that often go with rental properties. He found himself owning seven rental units, most of which he had never seen since he was a teenager. He had a full time repairman on the payroll and all went well for a while.

He had finished telling me about his day when I found myself asking, "Bob, when are you ever going to retire?" His answer was brief, as usual, and very much to the point.

"Never!" "I give Les credit for teaching me good work ethics and how to give my clients my personal attention. I will go by his rules as long as I live." We spent some time reminiscing about Les, and Little Tony and Jan and several others from the club that had left lasting impressions with both of us. When I left him that day, I was filled once again with admiration for this 'Quad' (as he always referred to himself) who had such a great sense of loyalty and unconditional love for all his fellow men.

One day, he realized that instead of his being the owner of seven houses they were instead beginning to own him. One by one, he started to dispose of them. In most cases he sold them to the people who had been renting them. He said, for sentimental reasons, he could never sell his mother's old home, behind his new house, and he hated to sell the one next door as he had allowed the man who kept up his yard to live in it.

Bob felt sorry for him as he had been a person without employment and no place to live when they first met. Bob took personal pleasure in watching him begin to take pride in himself, as he became a man with a job and with a home and enough money in his pockets to take care of his own needs. Bob let him live in one of the little houses he had bought next door and instructed him on things he must do. Topping the list, he must take care of the little garden his mother had planted in the front yard. She always kept it pretty with blooming flowers for Bob to enjoy when he was working in his office.

His zest for living was often evident by the times when he was placed on his left side and could look out his beautiful picture window and watch the birds fighting over the bird feeder that his mother had put within his view. He remembered complaining when she had planted big leaf elephant ear plants and philodendrons just outside his window. They grew too big too fast, he often had told her, but as he spent hours on the respirator he was able to see little green spring frogs hopping from leaf to leaf. I often wondered if he, in his wonderful mind, played leapfrog with them.

He enjoyed the flowers that changed with each season, the same flowers his mother had planted by the birdbath. All of this beauty was a constant reminder of his mother and the many sacrifices she had made for him through the years. She had truly been *The Wind Beneath His Wings*.

Bob was always so pleased when his visitors made comments about his yard. He was proud to have his own gardener and spent many hours just talking with him in the evenings. Bob supervised from his bed all changes in the yard, putting special emphasis on keeping the flowerbed his mother had planted at the front door. He especially loved and enjoyed seeing the Easter lilies come into bloom each year, as they had been gifts to him through the years. When their blooms had died off, his Mom had planted each one of them in her garden so Bob could continue to enjoy them.

It was easy for me to see that Bob thought his time was running out. Our conversations were less jovial and much more serious. He surprised me one day when I had stopped in for just a quickie visit on my way home from work." I have something for you and you can do whatever you please with it." He called for his nurse to get a package from his bedroom.

When I asked if I could open it now, he had answered quickly, "Of course."

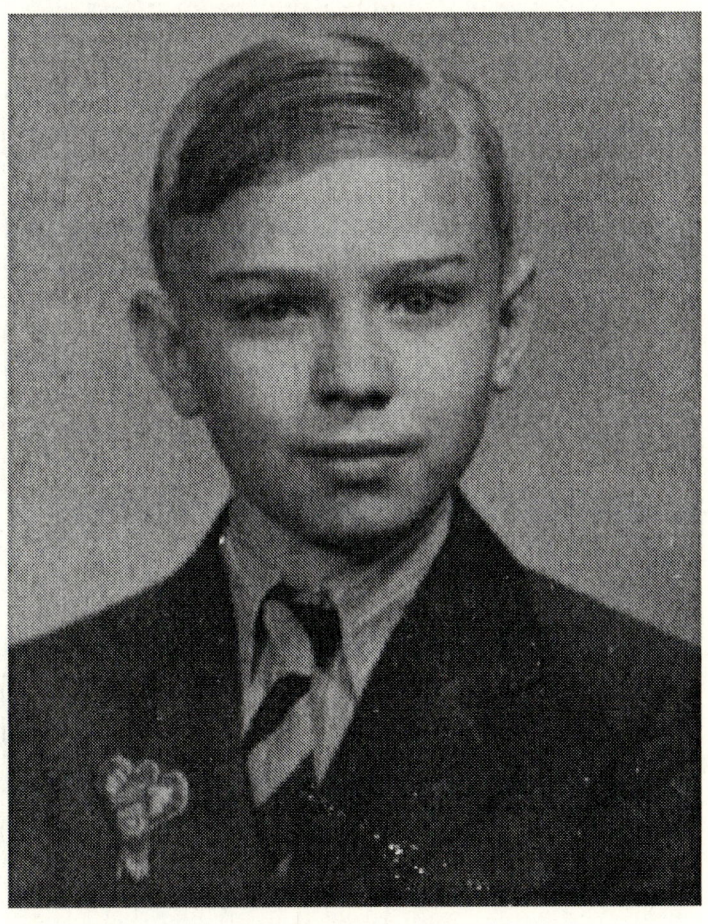

~Bob Baker at age 9~

When I removed the wrappings from the package, I found an 8/10" picture frame with narrow brass trim. A little boy, dressed in full suit, looked up at me.

The big blue eyes and half smile seemed to say "Hey, look at me. I'm Mr. Bob Baker."

I looked first at the picture and then at Bob. I saw the "little boy" inside the large still body of the sixty-five year old man lying on the bed. "What a darling picture," I exclaimed. "How old were you?"

"I was about nine years old, I think."

"Why were you so dressed up?"

"Mom saved and skimped to buy that suit. I was going to join the church and she said I had to look just right for the occasion. To her, it was worth the sacrifice." He looked wistfully at the picture and continued. "I want to give you the picture, Dottie. I don't care what you do with it, but somehow it upsets me to think it will go in the trash pile after I am gone. It was my Mom's greatest treasure in life and she always showed it off every chance she could. Now that she is gone, it seems to have become one of my dearest possessions too. Just take it with you, please, and keep it safe until after I'm gone. After that, I guess it won't matter to me what you do with it." His eyes filled with tears and I clutched the picture to my heart.

"Oh, thank you, Bob. I will treasure it forever." I said, wiping the tears from my own eyes. Already I realized that Bob was getting ready to leave us. And this was just one more step toward getting his life in order before the impending day of his departure from us.

"I'm in an awkward position, Dottie. Having no family who would want to keep items like that makes one wonder just what I should do with it." I found myself stroking his head with one hand and holding the picture with the other. Finally, I bent over and kissed him on his forehead. His eyes clung to mine, thanking me for being there for him.

"And Dottie, there is one other thing I would like you to have. You know the beautiful needlepoint picture Mother spent one entire year making, while sitting at my bedside? Could you possible use it? Or do you have someone who would like it?"

"The picture you sent to your Mom in the nursing home? Do you mean the one with the old lady and the cat?"

"That's it." He quickly said." Mom had already finished the needlepoint when together we thought that the picture needed a picture of a cat in it. Using our cat as her model she set about working the cat into the picture. We had a lot of laughs about that through the years and neither of us ever forgot how the cat came to be in the picture."

"Yes, I know the one you are talking about. What a lot of work! And yes, Bob, I would dearly love to have it. But I could get it later."

"Oh, no," he exclaimed. "I want to have the pleasure of giving it to you with warm hands, instead of..."

"Goodness Bob, I would be so very proud to hang it in my home." I quickly told him. "Not that I would ever need something to remind me of you. Our lives have been and always will be so closely entwined that there is no way I could ever forget you."

Dorothy Brosch

He called the nurse to go get the needlepoint picture for me and I left as soon as I possibly could clutching the two most treasured possessions of Bob's life.

26

In his eighth year on the respirator, Bob was besieged with a new set of maladies almost weekly. His doctor forbade him being off the machine but once a day for two hours or less, according to his daily reports from his nurse. He resisted the doctor's orders whenever he could. The hospital represented a double-edged sword for him. It could save his life, "if" he could stand being there. The sensory overload, sleep deprivation, change in routine and medical imbalance would often cause Bob to become paranoid and to hallucinate while he was in the hospital. It was his own personal hell, but even visits to the hospital could not eliminate Bob's sense of humor.

Once, after being admitted to Intensive Care and several attempts and much inflicted trauma to get a Central IV line placed in his chest, a nurse entered his room and informed him that she had to ask him some "standard questions." She read from a pre-ordained list, asking the most absurd one, given Bob's condition. "Do you have any special concerns at this time?"

Bob smiled wryly at her and said without a hint of sarcasm, "Concerns? No, I don't have any concerns. Do you?"

Months later, when the doctor was checking him at home, he cautioned Bob about working too hard as he was continually trying to stay on top of things happening in his office.

"I have to go to work," Bob argued. "My insurance policy is kicking in so far, but I am getting calls once a month from the company checking to see if I am still alive. I think they enjoy picking my brain to see how much longer I would need all this expensive equipment. They were too tactful to ask how much longer I was going to live, but their personal questions make me think that is what they meant. I have lost my temper with them a couple of times and they just might find some way to cancel my policy. Then, I would really be in a fix."

The doctor was listening intently but it was obvious hat he had other things on his mind.

"Whose cat is that?" he asked.

"That's my cat. His name is Shogun. He looks just like a cat I had when I was a little boy."

"I'm sorry to tell you Bob, but he has to go."

"What do you mean? He is the only family I have left," Bob declared, meeting the doctor's steady eyes.

"Sorry, Bob. Since you are on the ventilator, you simply cannot have that cat around."

Bob met his eyes defiantly, "No way, Doc."

"Well let me put it to you this way. Either the cat goes, or I go. It would take only one little sliver of dander in that trachea of yours, and you'd be a goner."

The nurse told me later that she could read Bob's mind as he contemplated letting the doctor go, but after mulling it over and thinking how long he had been his doctor and that he was the doctor who had kept the most complete medical record on him, she had seen Bob weakening.

"Oh, all right," he finally conceded. "Guess I will do what I have to do." The doctor gave him a pat on the head and an encouraging smile.

He looked at Bob with compassion as he was leaving. When he walked through the office to go to his car, he said to no one in particular, "What a guy!"

The Dear Frances Letter

Bob's eyes were clouded with tears when he told me later of the ultimatum the doctor had given him, and it was with misgivings that the nurse and I loaded Shogun into a cage and into my car with my promise to find him a good home.

The days and weeks marched slowly by in spite of the many phone calls and visits from friends and employees who did their best to help keep up his moral. He seemed to draw strength each time his secretary came in with the reports about his business. There were almost daily signs of improvement in his communication skills and slowly but surely, he was getting better. He was slowly adjusting to the purr of the respirator at his side. He was learning to control his breathing and attempts at speaking also improved.

Dorothy Brosch

～

Friends replaced his television set that sat on the floor with one on a shelf on the wall at his eye level. He became aware, one day, of the little bar scrolling across the bottom of the screen. He soon discovered that it was giving reports from the stock exchange. After hours on end of watching it, he thought there must be something he could learn from it. He became interested in the various stocks and it was not long before he started, in his mind, to buy some shares of stock.

As he continued day after day to watch it, he would decide when the time was right for him to sell. This became a daily hobby for him and he silently kept track of his winnings and of his losses. While telling me about it, he confessed to "winning a few and losing a bunch." Finally he had a winning streak, in his mind anyway, and this was most encouraging to him and the idea of investing in a little, real stock began to gnaw at him.

Bob became more and more interested in the stock market. "If I could afford to, I'd buy some stock for real. But I'm not ready yet to take such chances."

He learned to follow up on his make-believe purchases with the reports in the daily newspaper. Eventually he delved into the stock market He began studying various company's successes and failures. He was beginning to enjoy life again as he played with his stock and made a few more small investments.

On one occasion, he was considering upgrading his personal computer. My son Glenn, related the good experiences he and his associates had had with Gateway™

computers. Bob chose to buy a different computer from a local business who would install it for him. However, he was sufficiently impressed by his research into Gateway™ that he bought some of their stock, almost tripling his money in a remarkably short time! Similarly, he began studying Home Depot and made another opportune investment. By the time the technology stocks softened, Bob had invested in utilities, thus immunizing him from the big market drop.

"There are advantages" he said, "to having the time to study the market."

Bob continued calling his friends at night even though he was on the respirator. He let us do most of the talking as he lay in his bed, gasping for breath. He threw in a one-liner every now and then or a grunt at the appropriate time to let us know he was still with us.

There came a time when my phone would ring and when I answered, I would hear a single weak word : "Bible." I knew he wanted me to read to him. He seemed to receive solace and comfort most of all from *The Book of Psalms*. I could hear the purr of his machine, in the background, pumping away, supplying air to his lungs while I read chapter after chapter.

When he grew tired, I would hear him say in a weakened voice, "Thanks Dottie. Tomorrow?" and then I would hear the dial tone and hang up my phone.

The days when he was not well enough to have visitors became more and more frequent but we were kept informed by the kind nurses on duty. We heard the doctor was coming weekly now and talking with the charge nurse daily and more often as needed. One by one, all of his systems were shutting down. Along with his private duty nurses, either Jo Ann Harvey or Sherrie Dulworth was there for him as they had promised they would be when he needed them, especially during hospital stays. But this time was different. This time would be the last time.

Toward the end, Bob's mind was unwilling to let go, but his body was clearly failing. The doctor wanted Bob to be admitted to the hospital in early December because of a low level infection. Bob made his own decision, telling Sherrie and Jo Anne, "No more hospitals." The last couple of stays in the hospital had been torturous to him and he was very tired. He had made them promise that he could die at home. He had made the decision long before about how he would live until he died.

When he was allowed to have visitors, they could often be seen teary eyed and shaking their heads as they left his room. We all feared that this was the end of the road for Bob. His recovery was slow and labored, but he took heart each time he saw a new face in his room, especially when he recognized another dear friend. After all the guests had departed Bob told me how he had compartmentalized his friends. He admitted to loving and appreciating all of them, but there were five he felt he could not live without. He called them his extended family. I knew who they were before he named them as I had watched the deep love grow for each of them over the years and had observed his reactions when anything out of the ordinary happened to them.

The Dear Frances Letter

The five members of Bob's extended family were:

Sherrie Dulworth, who started working for Bob at age 17 as his part-time secretary, learning the insurance business and helping take care of Bob's personal paperwork. She became his "date" on many occasions when they attended concerts or just went out for sightseeing adventures. Perhaps the most treasured service, however, was to become his trusted friend, confidant and sounding board. Bob learned early in this relationship that he dearly loved this beautiful, blond, vivacious lady.

Later, when she faced career and college choices, he encouraged her to enroll in nursing school. After graduation, Bob continued to coach her to use her potential and be all that she could be. She went on from clinical nursing to the business world and worked in various positions including international work and in later years moved to New York in an executive position. Parting was painful to both of them, even though they stayed in close touch via telephone and occasional visits when she came home on vacation or holidays.

Bob had requested that Sherrie and Jo Anne be his health care surrogates. Sherrie, because she was an R.N., would speak with his doctor via long distance, and get back to Bob to further explain what she had learned and to answer any of his questions.

The mutual love and respect that they shared continued through the years with no amount of distance shaking this firm relationship that had grown between them.

Leah Dennis, a bubbly sophomore in high school, replaced Sherrie after she went off to nursing school. Bob soon grew accustomed to having Leah around and enjoyed the fresh enthusiasm she brought to his office each time she came. She was a sweet and caring person and capable of doing the job Bob had for her. He learned right off that he could trust her with money as well as confidences. He soon was calling her "His Girl Friday."

He watched her work ethics and was impressed with what he saw as she grew up under his watchful eye and graduated. He was not shy about telling his friends that she seemed like a daughter to him, the daughter he would never have. She found Bob to be a wonderful counselor and loved getting advice from him. Leah is very happily married now and cherishes the days spent with Bob.

~

Jo Anne Harvey, a red-haired social worker came into Bob's life to take over my position with the Recreation Department when I retired. She recognized from the start that Bob would be the key to her success with the club. She saw that he knew everything there was to know about the members, and she soon started reaching out to him for advice and guidance as she familiarized herself with her new duties.

Jo Anne was captivated by his charm and unusual knowledge about the needs and likes of everyone. She started taking her own mother to visit with Bob's mother on Sunday afternoons while she soaked up and enjoyed her down time with him. When she was visiting Bob one day, she was thinking of his many accomplishments and wondered out loud " With all that you have done, I can't help but wonder what you would have been, had your accident not happened."

He quickly answered, "I would have probably been a bum."

Jo Ann retired and is still working with her church and doing social work on a volunteer basis. She has always been proud to have served as one of Bob' health care surrogates and to have had him as her friend. She has many pleasant memories of the card games she and Bob, as partners, won out over their mothers.

~

Betty Kah, Stuart Kah's wife, leaned heavily on Bob for strength and methods to cope with her husband's protracted illness, and ultimate death. Bob's wisdom and broad experience continued to be a source of strength for Betty as she slowly made her way back into society and learned to make her own decisions about her personal life. Bob helped her to sell her home after Stuart died and advised her about how to go about finding another home to replace it. Betty and Stuart had lived in an isolated rural area for twenty years and now she agreed with Bob that she should have closer neighbors and live nearer to town for her own safety and convenience for medical help and shopping.

Bob guarded her possessively, offering comfort and advice every inch of the way. After several months of close personal and telephone contact, Bob confessed to me that he had fallen madly in love with her and was sorely tempted to ask her to marry him but he didn't feel strong enough to risk a possible "NO."

"She needs someone to take care of her," he told me confidentially. "And I need someone to share my life with and to take care of."

Betty was stricken with ALS one year after Bob's death and died just a short while later.

~

And lastly, there was me.

~My son, Gary Brosch, Bob, me on the right with Gary's daughter, Jessie.~

The Dear Frances Letter

I enjoyed teasing Bob about his many loves and accused him of having a heart as big as his body.

He chuckled and answered, "I'm a lucky guy, and Dottie, I've always heard the person who has five people in his life that he can call true friends is a successful man. Well, I can go one step beyond that as I can boast of having five true and faithful loves in my life, plus a business that has supported me and made my dreams come true." His smile spread from ear to ear.

27

We watched as Bob's health deteriorated. The doctor forbade any visitors for a few weeks, but on his few better days, we were allowed to just drop in for a few minutes to say hello.

It became more and more painful to say "good bye" to Bob when we visited him in his home and it was time to leave. We wondered each time if we would ever see him alive again. To add to our frustrations, Christmas lights were shining from all the neighboring houses and shoppers were seen coming and going with packages and laughter everywhere. Even the little Christmas tree on a table in Bob's office seemed to add to our sadness and anxiety.

Bob's staff and nurses and closest friends were able to visit him for a short while on the day before Christmas, but it was as if he had been waiting for Sherrie Dulworth to fly in from New York. She was with him only a few hours on Christmas Day when he released his final tenacious grip on life and drew his last breath. The respirator was turned off a short while later when the truth sank in and those with him had to face the fact that Bob Baker was actually dead.

When it was time to order flowers for his casket, someone remarked about how exceptionally beautiful the trees he had planted were. Both trees were laden with small white orchids. It was as if we were all in one mind

The Dear Frances Letter

and we went to his neighborhood florist and asked if they could make a blanket of orchids for his casket. Again, we listened to a long tale about how Bob was always ordering flowers for his friends or someone he felt needed a little beauty in their lives. The stories of the day were endless, leaving us completely drained when it was time to go home.

The Tampa Tribune ran a two-column article the next day after Bob died, entitled: "Paralyzed, he moved more than most of us."

They quoted one of Bob's pet philosophies: "We are not judged in this life by the size of the things we accomplish, but by the size of the things we allow to knock us down".

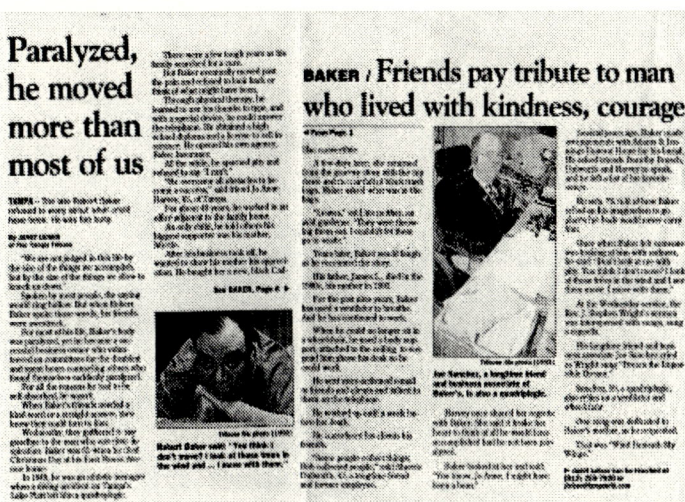

The article, written by Janet Leiser of the *Tribune*, went on to say, "For all the reasons he had to be self-absorbed, he wasn't."

I'm certain that Bob would be happy to know (and perhaps he does) that all of his favorite songs he had selected more than six years earlier, were sung at his funeral and that the beautiful trees he planted so many years ago, had provided a very beautiful mass of orchids to blanket and cover his casket. His beautiful cat, Shogun, continues to rule my home along with my little dog, Jasper.

He would be pleased to know too that Jan finished business school and was hired on with the Veteran's Administration to work in the office. She met the love of her life and was a happily married woman until her death from a heart attack on August 17, 2004. (Of course, maybe Bob already knows this too.)

We had a call from the funeral home asking us to be at Bob's house before the funeral, as they would be sending a car to transport us. We were waiting when a long black limo pulled into the driveway. There was an outburst of shock as someone asked, "What in the world is that for?" I found myself smiling as I recalled the time years before, when Bob had set this up for his extended family.

As we climbed into the limo, we were almost freezing. The temperature had not only dropped but the limo driver had forgotten to turn the heater on. Sherrie, Jo Ann, Betty, Leah and I were almost overcome with grief. Each of us was suffering in our own way, making conversation impossible as we boarded.

Suddenly, I looked to my right and there on a small shelf that had been pulled from the wall was an ice bucket holding a large bottle of Champagne. I had to cover my mouth to keep from laughing I pretended I had not seen it. And I thought to myself "You did it, you Rascal. You got the last laugh after all!"

EPILOGUE

It was weird going into Bob's house the next day with the respirator still there and his empty bed all made up - and no Bob. A heavy gloom had settled over everything. Even the weather depicted sadness, very cold and dark as if someone had turned off the lights. We divided the names and phone numbers in Bob's little black address book that he had always kept by his side, so we could call and tell his friend's about his passing.

Some of the stories we heard while doing this were very sad but it was amazing how many remembered a funny joke Bob had pulled on them in the past.. There was the elderly couple that had been Bob's neighbors years ago and he had remembered them each year with a box of Florida oranges. Some said they were fearful that he was not doing well since for the first time in years they hadn't received a Christmas greeting from him. Another was an elderly woman who had recently lost her husband but before he died, Bob had sent him a large magnifying glass so that he could read his paper in the mornings.

I know there are many others whose lives Bob Baker touched. And for those of you who never knew Bob during his lifetime, I can only hope that this book has provided you with a taste of his boundless love and his refusal to allow any physical limitation to become a liability.

Bob Baker wrote 42 letters to special people in his life some six or seven years prior to his death. While I was not privy to the other 41 letters, I do have the letter that he wrote to me.

Here are some excerpts from my letter. In sharing these, I hope to give you a glimpse of the compassionate nature of this remarkable man.

Dear Dottie

I saved your letter for last. I just did not know where or how to begin, but let me try to make some sense of things.

You were the one. You saved my life. Everything I am and everything I have…all of it is because of you. Diligent and stubborn Dottie, you just wouldn't let me be a poor helpless quad, would you!

How on earth did you ever contend with my anger! You are my Mother Theresa. Do you also know that because of you my mother had some measure of peace in her life. My mother <u>knew</u> you would be here long after she was gone to watch over me.

…

And as for you Dottie, you are the very air I breathe. My life is so wrapped up in yours and I <u>know</u> I simply would not want to continue on if you were not in this world.

Our daily phone calls…morning and night… what a boon to my existence! Just like taking your morning vitamin!

There are so many things I want to tell you, and to thank you for. You know, our relationship is constantly evolving. You have been my friend, my mother, my child, my lover, my teacher, my restrainer, my care-giver, and my cook (!!!). You have been all those things at one time or another. And you also adopted Shogun!!! I mean, that's a real friend!

How I cried for you when Ray died. How I cried for you at the loss of your sister, your mother, and even your little grandbaby. My arms were around you at every juncture! And they always will be, long after I make my grand exit from this planet.

You know, I have an inner circle of intensely protective friends. But if you only knew the depth of my love for you Dottie!! You are the one! You always have been!

You have brought life and light into my world in so many ways. Remember when you convinced me to put in the window in my room. What a difference that made to me. I could see God's creation in all of its glory.

. . .

The way you have always allowed me to share in your life has added years to my life. Your two fine boys, Gary and Glenn, often I imagined them as my own two sons.

. . .

More than all of this, Dottie, I am leaving you the largest part of my heart. I will <u>always</u> love you. It has been my good fortune to know you and to have you in my life.

You are the one, Dottie. You always have been the one.

Love,

Bob

P.S. Don't cry for me. I'm dancing on the clouds now...maybe even playing a little soccer.

Appendix – The Letter

August 6th, 1996

My dear Frances,

It has been my intention to bring you up to date on these many years in the form of a brief auto-biography... But the time has passed and a few infections have come and gone and my words are still running around in my head... Anyway, here goes my best (if brief) efforts using a voice activated word processor called DragonDictate!

We first met in April, 1949, when I was just 15 plus a few months. (See photo No. 1) I stayed at ol.' Tampa Municipal Hospital for seven months, most of it on your floor. Then came the time to leave and you see the newspaper clippings showing that sad event. Sad because I did not know what was in store for me. (See photo 2) I should have been prepared to get the "reality check" of my life!

There were many things that happened at the hospital in St. Petersburg that have had a profound and continuing effect on my life, but I won't bore you with all the details in this letter. The most important one however, was the removal of my right kidney in 1951. By the time it was diagnosed, stones had destroyed the function and it could not be saved. The very good part was that Dr. Hewit [he was with Dr. Gilmer] performed the operation and I never had a moments problem with it again! I don't even know it's not there

After 13 months in St. Petersburg, I was discharged into the real unknown! Coming home was very scary! Mom did not know much about taking care of me, but she gave it her very best... And continued doing so for the next thirty-five years.... (There is a whole book to be written about this dedicated lady, but that will come later.)

2

At this point, I must pause and give you a tiny glimpse of my "state of mind" at that time It was Christmas eve 1950 when I was discharged from the hospital in St. Petersburg (dumped out, would be a more accurate description)

I was 16 with very little past, almost no present and (from my point of view) absolutely no future. No real education! No money! No goals! And, no way visible to attain any of these things.

In the next five years or so, I tried to finish highschool by correspondence study, but without a goal that resulted only in a GED diploma. (See photo #3) I tried a number of other things without much success—--and in the spring of 1956 a very fortuitous and wonderful thing happened!

I was invited to join a recreation group for handicapped people and there I met a wonderful and enthusiastic woman whose name is Dorothy Brosch . (There will be a lot more about this amazing lady in future letters, but that part of my story will fill another whole book by itself) Just by chance, she introduced me to Les Rosenblatt who was to become my first business associate - and over the next twenty years went on become a strong friend, a wise mentor and would help me form most of my basic business philosophies.

Another Business associate, Joe Sanchez, was also brought into our small group by Les Rosenblatt. Joe and I formed Baker-Sanchez & Associates, Inc. in 1965 and our 31 year association has been profitable and enjoyable. We have had some exciting experiences, both business and social. You can read about some of his many accomplishments in the previous article and the small one enclosed

Les was also a quadriplegic who took me under his wing and taught me about insurance and instilled most of my strong and correct business practices. The business principles I learned from him served me very well to this day. He is mentioned prominantly in the previous article I sent you.

The insurance business has been very good to me and provided a most comfortable income for most of these thirty eight years—I can hardly believe it has been that long.

In the late '50s and early '60s I started buying some small real estate, in my own neighborhood at first, and then gradually ventured into other nearby areas. This has proven to be an interesting, and sometimes profitable endeavor. This happened very gradually over the years, but at one time I had as many as 8 houses, plus a 7 unit apartment house. It turned out that some of these properties "had me" and not nearly all of them were profitable. I have disposed of all of these houses except a few rentals that are located right in my neighborhood. They continue to be a serious problem at times, so I will be selling as soon as practical. I still have the old family home on the next street that was mostly built by my mom. That will probably be the last, and most painful, to part with.!

During the 1970s, I was involved in local politics in a minor way. As you can see by the enclosed letters, my involvement was very small, but most enlightening! My work with the Hillsboro County Democratic Committee was mostly "smoke filled room" type stuff and not very exciting. However, work with the steering committee was truly gratifying. Mr. William McInnes was the President of the Exchange Bank and President of Tampa Electric Company at that time and he was a real trip to work with—in most ways he acted just like an ordinary working man. However he was a very powerful man andclearly meant business!"

For all that work (very little of it was the result of my efforts) we now have a very large and highly respected rehabilitation center adjacent to TGH. I was finally able to go through the center in 1987 they were not able to do much for me, but it was most gratifying to see such a magnificent facility for helping people with all types of medical problems needing rehabilitation. There is even a heliport so that severely injured people can be brought right to the very entrance.

****

Here it is October 26th and nearly three months have passed since I started this letter. My comments bring me only up to about 1980s and there is much to tell since then, but I shall save those comments for another time, if you are still interested.

My very best to you. You have been in my thoughts so many times over these long years and you have no idea how much your inspiration meant to me in those terrible days so long ago.

These clippings and photos are yours to keep. Some are the originals and you are the only one to remember.

With great affection and admiration, I am

Sincerely yours.

About the Author

Dottie Brosch, a raconteur par excellence, spent many years as a recreation director specializing in working with handicapped persons. Her second career of directing activities in nursing homes began much later after her husband's death. She is known for her infectious positive attitude that has motivated many lives, and for that ever present twinkle in her eye. She is shown here with her dear friend Bob Baker. Dottie first met Bob when he was "...21 or 22, I guess" and became his loyal friend and one of his trusted "extended" family members.

The "Dear Frances" Letter is a labor of love, written to honor the memory of this valiant, unstoppable man, who refused to allow his severe physical challenges to get in the way of an outstanding, fruitful life.

Grateful for this 40-year friendship, Dottie is a story teller who grabs the reader in the very first sentence. It was always her intention to get Bob's story told, and now, shortly after celebrating her own 80th birthday, she celebrates Bob's life with this biographical book.

Dottie makes her home in Tampa, Florida where she lives a wonderful life with her little dog Jasper, and Bob's cat Shogun.

Printed in the United States
27085LVS00001B/136-219